A Field Guide to Everyday Life

A Field Guide to Everyday Life

Useful ways to reconnect with nature and humanity

By A.D. Anderson

Acknowledgments

The journey of everyday life does not leave us in one place to rest, but like a swiftly moving brook, sweeps us to new vistas of beauty and fruition for discovery and appreciation.

This book is dedicated to you and your journey. Thanks for the good things you are doing to make the world a better place.

Thanks to the many voices that came together in this special venue:

Esperanza Altamar	Luz Elena Anguiano	Kathryn Bonney
Dr. Jerry Cain	Lee Cain	Kim Compton
Sondra Elkins	Rabbi Chase Foster	Patricia Hill
Anne Hunter	Rev. Dr. Zina Jacque	Jim Kleinwachter
Laura Knoerr	Richard Louv	April Magill
Kay McKeen	Adele Moore	Jean Muntz
Stephen Packard	Candy Paull	Wendy Paulson
Chad Pregracke	Dr. Mike Rechlin	Dr. Noel Rudie
Dr. Benjamin Santer	Mary Schweinsberg	Debra Shore
Gary Swick	Dr. Douglas Tallamy	Jonathan Wright

Special thanks to Tom Voegeli for layout, design, and patience with the process.

Contents

Preface

Everyday Life is requires participation. So let's get started!

§   Make a difference

- Read a page of this book each day.

- Strive to learn from others. There are wonderful people who are doing amazing things right where you are and a wealth of literature devoted to this subject.

§   Plant seeds

- Nurture good ideas as well as a can-do attitude.

- Volunteer in your community and demonstrate environmental stewardship in everything you do.

§   Take care

- Eat well. Choose food that is naturally beautiful, flavorful and healthy for energy and strength. Grow and share food with others.

- Be active. Exercise your mind and body in everything you do each day.

Introduction

Naturalists use field guides to identify birds, rocks, and wildflowers, as well as various other living and non-living things. Field guides provide interesting facts, and illustrations to help an eager learner grow in his/her appreciation of nature.

While this field guide won't tell you the difference between *Echincacea pallida* and *Echinacea purpurea*, it will provide a framework for you to consider your experiences as they relate to the natural world and humanity.

This book is not designed to be another chore in an already activity-laden day, but a springboard for taking positive action and a joyful refuge for you to record ideas as well as amazing moments in time to share with others or hold in your heart. Each page has been crafted to stand alone, so you can freely move to topics that resonate with you each day.

Everything good, joyful, pure, and naturally beautiful is what makes everyday worth living. In the sections titled *Unraveling the Nature of Humanity* and *Practicing Harmonious Living* you are invited to embrace wonder and soar to new summits of thought and revelation anywhere you happen to be.

Unraveling the Nature of Humanity

Signs and wonders

Did you know… "Signs and wonders" are mentioned 14 times in The Holy Bible (KJV)?

I was sitting in church one day when I heard "… except ye see signs and wonders, ye will not believe." (John 4:48) "Signs and wonders," I pondered, what did the writer mean? Was he talking about a once-in-a-lifetime occurrence or something that we discover anew each day? Is it not amazing that we have light and stars? Rocks and trees? Birds and flowers?

Earth is a tiny speck in the cosmos, yet for most of us, it will be the only home we will ever experience. While signs and wonders may sound like the relics of biblical times, they persist today if we're open to them.

What does the natural world have to teach you today? Snowflakes show us how many ice crystals can transform a dreary scene into a beautiful landscape. Daffodils signal the arrival of spring and brighten the yard with their sunny hues. Western chorus frogs, another harbinger to spring, sing loudly to find mates after the last of the ice has melted. Sandhill cranes circle overhead, their gargling voices heard more often than their distant circle seen.

§   Approach each day with a sense of childlike wonder.

- Get outside and look at the sky, the birds at a backyard feeder or the persistent dandelion in the sidewalk. Turn over a rock and see what is living beneath it. How do the lives of other creatures inspire you?

- Share the wonder of your nature discoveries with family and friends. Each year, my father-in-law and sister-in-law (his daughter) have a contest to see who will see the first robin of spring. Every time we travel, my family listens to me get excited about a tree that we don't have in our area, a bird I've only seen in books, lichens covering great rocks, wildflowers, rainbows, and more.

Draw or write about or what you see with your heart.

Patience

One fall, my son found a cocoon lying in the grass. It was a neat tan mass of leaves that resembled a thick thumb, so I put it in a screened bug box to share with my students, being careful to keep it outside so it wouldn't hatch prematurely.

It overwintered in an unheated garage and showed no signs of life. As spring approached, I didn't want to tell my son that I thought the pupa was dead, so I didn't mention it. I thought he might forget about it, too; but he didn't. With each warming day, he expected it to hatch, yet with each passing day, there was no discernible sign of life. By this time, I had brought the bug box into the house, expecting to put the cocoon outdoors within the next day or two.

As I was washing the dishes, I was distracted by the movement of what appeared to be a large brown leaf in the bug box on the counter. It flailed about in its restrictive confines as I marveled.

The cocoon had opened, and there was a moth the size of my hand. As I opened the lid of the box, the moth did not immediately fly away, but allowed me to gently pick it up and release it outdoors.

➤ Cultivate patience with yourself and others by striving to express joy and gratitude.

- The unfolding wings of a moth or butterfly preparing for its first flight illustrate the intricate relationship between patience and progress. Consider how your life is unfolding new opportunities to discover perfection through goodness and grace.

- Be happy wherever you are – whether you are stuck in traffic, waiting in a line, or trying to resolve a challenge in your life. Bring a sense of joy (maybe even a little humor) to the situation.

Write about something that is requiring you to develop patience and share ways you are working to nurture this quality in your life.

Watch sunlight reach through the clouds

Draw something you've observed and share thoughts you've associated with this event (the movement of a honeybee from flower to flower, an autumn leaf falling from a tree, a snowflake descending to a drift on the ground, etc.).

Date: _______________________

Music

Did you know... Chipmunks chirp like birds to claim territory, alert others to danger and attract mates?

"BOOM, Ba-Ba-BOOM" blasts the bass stereo of a passing car. "Cheer, Cheer, Cheer," sings a male cardinal from a nearby tree. A flute-like robin voice joins the chorus. A toad hops off the path. A unique combination of rhythms and sounds invites our exploration.

➢ Listen.

- Go outdoors at different times of the day each month, close your eyes, and listen. How many different sounds do you hear? What is their source?

- Look for the origin of the sounds you hear. Visit your local library or get online to find resources for bird, frog, even insect song identification.

- Visit a park or zoo to make more discoveries.

Take a moment to reflect about the sounds you hear and how they make you feel.

____

____

____

____

____

____

____

The cry of the crane
Echoes in the foggy sky
Asking me to join

— Kim Compton, Naturalist

Laws of nature

Principles or laws guide our daily lives.

Governed by the laws of the road, I know that I must keep my vehicle within certain boundaries – be it a bicycle or a car – but what I find most curious is how everyone else does the same, moving at speeds unimaginable in the narrow confines of a road or path.

This is not to say that lines are never crossed and fenders are never bent, but that for the most part, countless vehicles move in amazingly sharp lines – like ant lines to food or bees around a hive. Order is the way of nature and the foundation for harmonious living.

- ➤ Observe the orderliness of the natural world and reflect it throughout your day.

- Strive for balance in all things – work, school, family, and play time.

- Let your day take a natural path, progressing from one activity to another with joy rather than resistance.

Draw what you see over the course of four observations of the same place in the four boxes below..

<table>
<tr><td>

</td><td>

</td></tr>
<tr><td>

</td><td>

</td></tr>
</table>

Sorting beans

One day I was visiting my friend while she was getting ready to cook beans.

I thought nothing of the task, as I had done it many times myself, but my friend took a different approach. After carefully washing and straining the beans, she took small handfuls of beans and scanned them for impurities, picking out tiny clods of dirt as well as beans that didn't measure up. I thought about how I had always rinsed and dumped my beans, figuring I'd notice any rocks as I was pouring the wet beans into the cooking pot. It made me wonder how many undesirable bits of bean and debris I had carelessly permitted to enter.

Today, I cooked some more beans, but before I got started, I took my friend's watchful approach.

> ➢ Be as picky about your attitude, friends, activities, and time, as beans in a pot!

- How many thoughts or actions do you let go by every day without questioning them? Are they are all good? If not, why accept them?

- Focus on the beans (positive things in your life) and remove the clods of dirt (negative thoughts that would usurp your joy).

Use this space to write about the "beans" in your life and how you are removing the "dirt."

____

____

____

____

____

____

____

Shifting paradigms with a watermelon

When my kids were in elementary school, my son was in Cub Scouts with another boy from the neighborhood, so we often carpooled to save time and energy.

One day when I came to pick up the boy and his mom for a potluck picnic, the mom was putting away groceries. As she hurriedly finished putting one bag away, she didn't realize that the watermelon she was planning to take to the picnic was being supported by one of the other bags.

All I could do was helplessly watch as the watermelon rolled off the table and shattered inside the grocery bag. We were already running close on time. "What are we going to take to the picnic now?" I asked. "We're not going to have time to stop at the grocery store, and even if we did, we would still have to cut the watermelon."

The mom did not seem worried. She simply picked up the bag, looked inside, and said with a grin, "Great! The watermelon is already cut into pieces. Now all we have to do is cut the bigger pieces, and place them into a bowl."

Remembering that event, I tell myself not to worry. A good attitude always helps us see life in a positive light.

— Luz Elena Anguiano, Educator

Surface tension

Did you know... Cohesive forces between different molecules on the surface of water are responsible for creating surface tension?

At the community college, there is a beautiful indoor pond filled with lush plants, small fish, big-headed tadpoles, and fire-bellied frogs. I discovered the pond one day as I was going from one building to another and have always enjoyed taking my children there while visiting colleagues at the college.

Each time I visit, the pond is different – the last time there were more tadpoles, while this time, there appeared to be more plants. Both times I could not help but notice acrobatic snails moving upside down beneath the clear pudding-like surface of the water while water striders effortlessly glided across the top, exposing the invisible realm of surface tension.

- Let go of limitation and fear so you can move forward with confidence like a water strider

- Do something you've never done – something that's good for you, and the environment.

- Integrate positive feelings from this experience into your every day life.

Write about an experience in which you dealt with a feeling of limitation or fear, then share how you moved forward. Consider another challenge you'd like to address and how you might use what you've learned.

Volcanoes (and pigs) within

*Did you know... Scientists classify about 1,900 volcanoes on Earth as "active" because they show some level of activity?**

In a book titled *General Billycock's Pigs*, author Joan Balfour Payne spins a curious tale about a general with a terrible temper whose farm becomes plagued by like-minded swine. As the wild pigs destroy his crops, the general's health begins to deteriorate. His daughter Betsy leaves the farm to look for help and meets "an old Indian" who tells her that the general must "cast out the pigs from within."

Much like a volcano spewing hot lava, so hot tempers burn the ones we love, leaving devastation that is not easily repaired. Scientists estimate that hot lava can reach 2,000 degrees F or more and an erupting volcano can release ash and toxic gases, hurl boulders of hardened lava, and melt enough snow to bury a town.

- ➢ Purge yourself of anger and bitterness without spewing it on others.

- If you feel angry, get to the root of what's hurting you.

- Take a brisk walk or a deep breath to let off steam.

- Try to put yourself in the shoes of the other person.

- Find a way to laugh it off (without being sarcastic).

**Source: National Geographic*

Describe something you experienced that gave you a sense of peace when you were suffering with anger or bitter feelings. What are some positive ways to avoid spewing anger or bitterness on others?

____

____

____

____

____

____

Expecting good

Did you know... Self-fulfilling prophecy suggests that people have the ability create what they seek?

Rose, a woman who effervesces with enthusiasm, told me that she dreams of creating a business focused on employing individuals dealing with disabilities. It sounded like a noble cause and I could not help but share her excitement, yet I wondered about cash flow (the curse of a business background). "How are you going to pay the bills?" I asked.

Rose answered that she wasn't worried about the money, but that she expected it to follow. Her conviction was intractable, like a flower naturally unfolding its petals. Why should her life be any different than a flower? James Allen writes, "as the plant springs from, and could not be without, the seed, so every act of a man springs from the hidden seeds of thought, and could not have appeared without them."

- ➢ Grow in character, intelligence, beauty, and strength.

- Examine your expectations for today, tomorrow and the future, and root out the negative ones.

- Trust that even though you may not know the answer to a significant life question, the ideas you need are already present.

- Find something for which to be thankful and say "thanks."

Write about your expectations for unfoldment.

____

____

____

____

____

____

____

Sycamore

Did you know... It is hard to tell the exact age of a sycamore tree because their soft wood becomes hollow while they are still alive?

A giant sycamore tree stands beside a playground in a county park. Straight and stately, it stands several stories in height and so big around it would take at least five adults to completely encircle it. It was ghostly white with peeling brown bits of bark scattered randomly across its surface, trying to camouflage its brilliance in the varying shades of gray of a late November landscape.

It was not the remnant of a primordial forest like one might think, but about the age of a great-grandparent – 80-90 years old. While determining the exact age of a great sycamore is virtually impossible, perhaps it is a reminder to us that knowing the exact age of anything is really irrelevant.

> ➤ Look beyond age and learn from everything.

- All living things reflect order, growth, and development. Plant a seed and watch it grow. Compare this small plant to a bigger tree.

- Can you see a tree grow? Take a photo in the winter, then another in a year from the same vantage point. While you may not have noticed it, the tree continued to grow.

Not all growth is noticeable, but all progress should be celebrated. Record small ways you are growing as a person. Include things you'd like to do, too.

____

____

____

____

____

____

____

Sand

Did you know... Sand has been used for centuries to tell time? It doesn't evaporate or spill like water.

Taking a closer look at the coarse brown sand in the volleyball pit at the park, I see amazing diversity in the color, shape, and size of the particles that make up the whole. What initially appeared to be a blanket of brown reveals tiny black, red, white, and translucent rocks sparkling from a recent rain shower.

Each grain has a brilliant role, like a beautiful star in galaxy of a billion lights.

In some ways, we are not so different from these tiny bits of rock, broken apart by the harshness that surrounds us and transformed into something new and far greater when combined with others.

> ➤ Think about your relationship with the larger sphere of humanity.

- Consider how essential each small grain of sand is in building a home or road.

- Take a moment to consider the qualities your "grain" contributes to enriching humanity.

List the needs you see in your community, country, and world along with ways you can address these needs through your actions.

____

____

____

____

____

____

____

Good growing conditions

If you've ever nurtured a houseplant or cultivated a carrot, you know that every plant has special growing requirements – soils where they can make themselves at home, unique water and light preferences, and adversaries (such as pests, weeds, fungus or mold) which threaten to undermine their longevity.

My mom always put water in a little dish beneath her African violets, so they wouldn't get soggy stems or accumulate troublesome minerals around the edge of the pot. More than once, she'd get additional violets from friends who'd want her to bring theirs back to life. She would nurse these dying plants back to health and return them to their caregivers with the expectation they had learned their lesson and would follow her instructions. Most of her friends tried to do the right thing by their plants, but would sometimes lapse back into their former habits.

Bad habits can be overcome through awareness accompanied by a conscious commitment to change. Consider the importance of taking care of yourself and addressing the bad habits that keep you from being happy and achieving positive goals.

> ➤ Cultivate wisdom and strength.

- If you cannot take care of yourself, you cannot begin to help others. Do something to nurture your own growth as a person – study something you've always wanted to learn about, try your hand at painting or some other artistic endeavor, and most of all, play!

- Look at the growing conditions of others. What do they need to grow? Kindness, firmness, stability, strength? Do something to contribute to their growth and experience the joyous dividends down the road.

Make a mini-collage to illustrate qualities that can help you better support growth in yourself and others.

The iridescent trail

Large tawny garden slugs live in the woods near my home. They lay tiny pearl-like eggs and leave iridescent mucous trails as they glide along their one muscular foot. Sometimes their sparkly trails cross, while other times they leave solitary lines that disappear beneath a log.

Each sparkling trail reminds us that we can take countless paths through life and make meaningful discoveries along the way.

> ➤ Feel awe.

- Admire something beautiful from the natural world.

- Think about what you can do to make the world a better place and do it.

Record what comes to you.

____

____

____

____

Draw something you beheld.

Perseverance

One day I received an e-mail entitled "The Daffodil Principle" which described a home in the mountains of southern California surrounded by daffodils. The photo accompanying the e-mail depicted so many bright yellow daffodils that the image looked surreal. It all began in 1957 when a woman named Gene Bauer beheld the beauty of her neighbor's daffodils and decided to plant some in her yard. She planted 50 the first year, then 500, 1,000, 10,000, and finally 35,000 bulbs in 1993. Their beauty lingered in my thoughts, brightening my heart one dank winter day. I forwarded the e-mail. *Source: The Daffodil Principle*, by Jeroldeen Edwards.

> Share something inspiring with another person today.

- Look for and celebrate goodness.

- Use the so-called "Daffodil Principle" to tackle insurmountable projects with hope and faith that they will get done little by little. Start today.

Set high goals but realize that the bigger the goal, the more persistence, dedication, focus, and sacrifice it will take to achieve it. Big goals are accomplished only by taking small steps, and it starts with a single, small action.

When I originally started cleaning up rivers, my goal was to find less garbage over time. Eventually, I hoped to work myself out of a job. I realize that we are not solving all the problems or necessarily saving American rivers – we're simply doing our part, just as I hope you're doing yours.

We are working on huge rivers with huge problems and, in the grand scheme of things, garbage is probably the least of them. Some of the bigger issues such as siltation, runoff, and invasive species are not as easily solved. But if we can bring thousands of people to the shore, put them in boats, expose them to the river, and have them become part of the solution to the garbage problem, then they'll come back feeling like they have a stake in the river.

We all make a difference, even if we don't intend to, and it's either negative or positive. My question to you is, how big a difference do you want to make?

— Chad Pregracke, Founder, Living Lands & Waters and Author of *From the Bottom Up: One Man's Crusade to Clean America's Rivers*

Set goals and write steps for reaching them

Cutting bait

Did you know... The phrase "fish or cut bait" was a term coined by a U.S. judge in 1853?

If you've ever been fishing, sometimes you hang onto a fish that really isn't meant for you to keep. You struggle to pull it in, then want to release it, but the hook is so deeply entrenched in your scaly counterpart that to remove it would mean certain death. Instead, you cut the line and let it go. You do it without a second thought because it's natural.

> - Follow the gut feeling that is leading you to improve your life.

- Sit quietly at a park or natural area or take a silent walk to reflect and consider the goodness embracing you right now.

- Go fishing and think about how cutting bait frees both you and the fish (when it has to be done).

Write or draw about what you'd like rather than what you need to change. List ways you can cut bait (leave behind the hooks in life) and "swim" in happiness.

I believe many people needlessly live with resentment, but that anyone can change. I did. Being physically debilitated as the result of a series of negative circumstances, I chose to embrace love and recovered from emphysema. At that time, the journey was not easy, but natural to me. It's all about spiritualizing thought. Looking for the positive releases the negative. "As [a man] thinketh in his heart, so is he." Proverbs 23:7

— Kathryn Bonney, Author of *I Am Worthy, I Am Healed*

A house made of paper

Did you know... Bald-faced hornets have to make new homes every year?

Beginning with a layer of cells where she can lay eggs, the queen constructs the nest by herself until her descendants begin to hatch. As more wasps mature, they gather and chew wood to construct additional paper egg chambers beneath a thin outer layer of a nest that may eventually surpass the size of a football.

While a well-ventilated house made of paper works in the summer, cold weather kills the colony and harsh winds wreck the delicately layered paper design over time. As spring returns, the queen must begin the colony anew. Hard work is natural and healthy for this industrious insect.

➤ Work like a hornet.

- Look at every living thing. Each one has a purpose, function, or job. Consider its contribution to the ecological make up of the place you call "home."

- If you do not feel like you have a purpose, consider the presents you bring with your presence – a good thought, a friendly smile, a sense of humor, and more. Share this goodness with others through friendship, volunteer work, and every day living.

Reflect on ways you can give more.

Just for fun

*Did you know... Laughter reduces the effects of stress?**

When was the last time you laughed? Laughing out loud for 10-15 minutes each day can burn 10–40 calories, improve mood, boost immunity, lower blood pressure, decrease blood glucose levels, and protect the heart.*
Having a sense of humor is natural. Consider how animals offer opportunities to share a chuckle. Nuthatches walk down trees headfirst, squirrels chase each other around trees, chipmunks stuff their little cheeks with seeds, and skunks spray bothersome meddlers.

> ➤ See the humor in your life and find a way to make this joy contagious.

- Be open to humor like a flower is open to sunlight. Absorb the joy all around and express it through a smile or laugh.

- Share a funny story or good joke with others. Avoid those that put others down.

**Source: Center for Disease Control*

Write or draw something funny in your journal today.

____

____

____

____

Beta in a bowl

Did you know... Betas (also dubbed "Siamese fighting fish") are freshwater fish from southeast Asia with territorial tendencies?

As I was waiting in line at the bank in the local mega-store, I noticed two fish bowls on the counter by the teller. One contained water and rocks while the other held a crimson beta fish with a comparable habitat. In the confines of a bowl that resembled the hand-sized globes at county fairs, the beta poked about the rocks looking for something – his eyes fixed curiously on the bottom of his immediate world.

Was he looking for a piece of food or a way back home? I don't know if he found what he was seeking, but by that time it was my turn to be helped.

- ➢ Get out of your bowl.

- While it is not physically possible for a beta to leave its bowl or water behind, it is good for us to grow by challenging our comfort zones and connecting with others.

- Look beyond appearances and do something for someone who seems to be dealing with physical, mental, social, or economic challenges. Volunteer to prepare food for distribution at a food bank, assist with activities at a local nursing home, or share your talents as an artist, writer, musician, a bicycle mechanic, and more. You have so much to give!

Create a list of groups of people you'd like to serve and contact your local chapter of the United Way for assistance or look up organizations you'd like to serve in the telephone book or on the internet. (See Resources at the end of this journal for more information.)

____

____

____

____

____

____

Neighbor to neighbor

My father was a grocer in Lovington, New Mexico, and expected his sons (including me) to help with sacking, stocking and regular cleanup around the store. Not only did he expect us to be cleaned and dressed in Sunday clothes every day, but we were to know the names of our customers and greet them warmly. Out of respect we were to call them Mr. or Ms. and never use their first names because it was too casual.

The most important sound to any human being is not that of the dinner bell or the local orchestra, but rather the sound of one's own name. I am glad I learned to sack groceries, stock shelves, mop spills and call people by name. After all, Jesus knows his sheep by name (John 10:14, 27) and that should be a model for all of us.

— Dr. Jerry B. Cain, Chancellor, Judson University

No matter where you live, you are part of something bigger. Neighbors are more than the people next door, they are friends, relatives, colleagues and people we serve, who enrich our lives by their mere existence. Nature is a quiet neighbor that surrounds us with beauty. Understanding and appreciating neighbors of all kinds makes life meaningful.

- ➤ Demonstrate humanity through your actions.

- Make new connections with people from different generational groups, backgrounds, and beliefs, and appreciate each other's uniqueness.

- Strengthen one connection each day through good communication and sincere compliments face-to-face.

- Volunteer to clean up local parks, restore natural areas, and feed the hungry where you live.

Write down some ways you can express kindness toward the many neighbors in your life.

____

____

____

Saying good-bye

I watched our big orange tabby cat sleep in his favorite spot on top of the green chair, wondering if he would wake up. Several months ago, an unusual lump appeared on his side. We thought it was an old injury, but the veterinarian indicated the growing mass was something else and that our friend would be leaving our home for another.

I bawled at the thought of his departure, not expecting him to go so soon. He was about 15 years old and though we hadn't had him since he was a kitten, he had become a special member of our family, howling for breakfast every morning, basking in sunbeams, snuggling with family members when they were sick, and serving as a kind host to all guests.

It was fall. The leaves were changing color, and getting ready to depart from their summer homes. I wasn't crying for them. Why cry for my cat? Could it have been that I just didn't know how to say good-bye? In his book, *The Fall of Freddie the Leaf*, Dr. Leo Buscaglia's characters help readers look at death from the perspective of autumn leaves.

> Express the qualities you loved in another through the life you live.

- Take time to reflect.

- Give yourself permission to heal.

Write about the happy times you've spent together and be grateful.

Practicing Harmonious Living

Sustainable relationships

Did you know... The U.S. Environmental Protection Agency (EPA) created "Everyday Choices: Opportunities for Environmental Stewardship" to promote sustainable approaches to land, air, water, energy, ecosystems and materials in 2005?

Sustainability is not some radical environmental concept, but a very logical way of addressing what we want now and for generations to come – a place where we can comfortably live and connect with something far bigger than ourselves.

It's about relationships with our neighbors, and the cosmos. It's about being conscious of the present, and how it relates to the future. Sustainability is love for nature and humanity that's put into action.

- ➤ Take steps toward living more sustainably.

- Reduce waste.

- Support local businesses.

- Volunteer.

Celebrate things you've done to improve your community and outline other things you'd like to start doing today.

If we, as citizens of the planet, are to cherish and care for our natural heritage, we need to know it firsthand. Urban nature sanctuaries give us that opportunity. A city that incorporates a tapestry of parks and natural habitats – including native trees along its streets and roadways, and community and school gardens – is a city that honors nature, that recognizes the sense of inquiry and wonder that encounters with birds and butterflies and bats inspire. It promotes wakefulness (Did you see that yellow-bellied sapsucker drilling holes in the locust along Columbus Avenue?); curiosity (Why are there other birds feeding at the holes, too?); gratitude (What a gift to be able to watch sapsuckers and warblers on my walk to work this morning!). Such a city honors its people, too. It recognizes the pleasure of learning, the delight of unexpected encounters, the pride in the beautiful.

— Wendy Paulson, Teacher & Conservationist

Tap a maple

Did you know... It takes about 40 gallons of sap to make 1 gallon of maple syrup?

In early March, buckets hang off sides of trees as plastic tubing traverses the forest in small maple groves scattered about rural Illinois.

If you lift the lid covering one of the buckets and gaze inside looking for an answer, you will only find something that looks like water. Like any great detective, you cannot abandon your search for an answer, so you follow the footprints in the snow (or plastic tubing) to a building with clouds of steam billowing out of its roof. You go inside the building (better known as a "sugar shack") and discover that this watery substance is really sugar maple sap being concentrated and transformed into a delectable, amber syrup.

You taste a sample and feel satisfied. This is not the thick maple-flavored corn syrup you put on pancakes at the church fundraiser, but real maple syrup, a natural sweetener derived from a tree in the forest – a food that carries you back to a simpler time.

> Give locally harvested food a try.

- Consume more whole and natural foods (rather than processed ones), so you can appreciate what generations before you have enjoyed and benefit from good nourishment. In addition to its satiating sweetness, maple syrup contains nutrients not found in other syrups.

- Try simple recipes using natural foods, and swap recipes with friends.

What can you make using whole or natural foods? Use the next page to record a favorite recipe (or two!).

In the waning days of winter, tapping trees to make maple syrup gets you outside, in the woods, appreciating nature. The smells and sounds of the evaporator, as you boil the sap to syrup, can be a magical time with family and friends sharing the workload. Then there is the satisfaction of the harvest. With the coming season's seed catalogs still in the mail, you are already putting food in your larder.

— Dr. Mike Rechlin, Author of *Maple Syrup: An Introduction to the Science of a Forest Treasure.*

Mmmmm

Use this space to record a few healthy, easy-to-make recipes using fruits, vegetables, and/or grains.

Corn and soybeans

Row after row of perfectly straight corn plants wave their broad leaves in the breeze. Soybeans grow in lush colonies on the other side of the road. Acres and acres of gently rolling farmland as far as the eye can see make a summer drive an opportunity to appreciate the amazing handiwork of farmers, machinery, and nature. From the machines that plant seeds to those which harvest crops, farmers possess tools that enable them to reap more food in a day than their ancestors could gather in a season.

Farming demonstrates the intimate relationship humans have with the earth. Cultivating and selling the fruits of their labor, farmers depend on weather, soil, seeds, and animals or equipment for their living. Nature permeates their everyday lives, comforting them with warm sunbeams and challenging them with strong winds, watering their crops, and offering dry times to harvest.

> - Acknowledge the relationship of humans to the vast natural world.

- Volunteer in a community garden or farm to experience the joy of cultivation and help provide food for others.

- Think about how you're helping the natural world while volunteering to clean up a local park or assist with trail maintenance.

Draw how you see your relationship to the natural world.

Poison ivy

Did you know… Poison ivy (Toxicodendron radicans) is classified as a vine, shrub, and herb by the US Department of Agriculture?

"I'm going to miss that poison ivy vine," I thought as I used a bow saw to cut through a hairy stem the thickness of two broomsticks clinging to a small tree. Each fall, I admired its beautiful peach-colored foliage, and warned visitors not to gather its leaves. The vine was not in my yard, but next to the driveway of a nearby nature center.

Volunteers had cleared invasive trees from the base of this tree (when the poison ivy was not out), so I became concerned that its pretty leaves would attract even more leaf pickers. It was time for the vine to be cut and treated with herbicide, so its host tree – a small white ash – would be free from the vine's parasitic influence. While looking pretty, the vine had bent an otherwise healthy sapling in half.

➢ Let go of the poison ivy in your life!

• Don't be duped by appearances. Like the pretty poison ivy leaves laden with vicious oils, appearances can be deceiving. Look deeper.

• Seek a greater sense of good in your life, by doing good things for yourself and others.

Write about the good things you are doing (or would like to do) for yourself and others.

____

____

____

____

____

____

____

Excuses

Once I visited a state park with no garbage or recycling containers – either at the trailheads or in the nature center. A sign where the containers formerly sat explained how this was helping the state cut its waste management costs.

As I hiked along the trail, I hoped that people would be responsible for their waste. Instead, I found water bottles, cans, wrappers and other debris strewn along the more accessible areas, and bits of scattered trash deeper in the forest.

Would the trash and recyclables have found their way to the correct containers at the trailhead if they had been provided? It's hard to say. One can always look for excuses, but litter is a menacing blight to the natural world.

➢ Pick up litter and recycle it whenever possible.

• Bring a bag and a pair of gloves to pick up litter where you hike, and encourage others to pick up after themselves.

• If recycling is not available, contact the National Recycling Coalition for information about how to start a recycling program in your community.

As I rounded a bend in the road, it was difficult to process what I was seeing. Our center had received a call about an owl stuck in a tree, but this one was hanging from a high branch by a piece of fishing line attached to its wing tip. Looking up at the motionless great horned owl, I hoped he hadn't suffered too much before his death, then wondered how we would get the body down. At this point, the owl opened his large yellow eyes and stared directly at me. He was alive!

My next thought was how we could capture the owl without causing the bird to struggle and further damage the wing. A bucket truck with the capability of reaching the bird was finally located and the owl was retrieved. Amazingly, the fishing line didn't cut off circulation to the wingtip or slice into his skin. After approximately six weeks of rehabilitation the owl was released back into his territory. Wildlife releases are always a mix of joy, excitement and hope, tempered by the reality that there are many more out there who still need our help, and are beyond our help.

Litter kills! Retrieve as much tangled fishing line as you can instead of leaving it lying around. When planning outdoor memorial services, think of ways to honor loved ones other than balloon releases. Balloons end up in trees and bushes where wildlife can become entangled. Caring for wildlife begins with injury prevention.

— Adele Moore, Co-Founder, TreeHouse Wildlife Center, Dow, Illinois

One man's trash is another man's treasure

Everything we do makes a difference. My husband and I got into the garbage and recycling business after I bought a backyard pony because it bothered me that all of her manure was going to a landfill. I thought, "there has to be a spot where this can be used."

Almost anything can be recycled if you find the right source. We recycle horse manure, cat litter, dog manure, food scraps, yard waste, Halloween pumpkins, broken Christmas lights, electronics, clothing, and gym shoes in addition to the cans, bottles, and plastic containers you'd expect a recycling service to remove. Animal waste, food scraps, and yard waste are sent to a composting facility. Clothing is either used secondhand, recycled into cleaning cloths, or reprocessed for fiber. Depending on their quality, gym shoes may be sent to people overseas or ground up to make soft surfaces for playgrounds and sports facilities. Plastic, glass, and metal go to a processing plant where they can be can be used to make new products.

I think if we knew how precious the environment was, we'd all be different people. Encouraging more people to care about reducing waste is our ultimate goal.

— Mary Schweinsberg, Owner/President PrairieLand Disposal and Recycling

86,400 seconds   1,440 minutes   24 hours

Did you know… About 50% of Americans feel that they don't have enough time in a day to do what they want?

No matter how you cut it, 86,400 seconds is 1 day. Family, work, school, volunteer commitments, recreation, religious, and wellness activities comprise about 2/3 of this time while the remaining third is generally reserved for relaxation and sleep. With so much to do, how can we find time to make our world a better place?

Determine your priorities. Tell your friends and colleagues so they can encourage and support you.

- ➤ Make a conscious choice to use time wisely.

- Do two things at once – Ride your bicycle or walk wherever you can, so you can enjoy the benefits of fresh air, fitness, and economical transportation.

- Encourage family and friends to join you in work, recreation, religious, and volunteer activities to enjoy reaching goals together.

Keep this book where you can see it every day and track your progress with words and/or drawings.

____

____

____

____

Take a break from watches, cell phones, and other technology for a day or weekend

What is it like to be unplugged from watches, cell phones, and other technology? Describe how it feels to reconnect with nature using poetry, prose, collage, or other forms or art.

Date: _______________________

One fast squirrel

Did you know... Squirrels can run 8–10 miles per hour?

A four-lane road is not a place you want to see wildlife, but some patchy oak woodlands, farm fields, and wetlands along the edges still serve as wildlife habitat for a surprising number of birds, bugs, and occasional squirrels.

One day as I sat at a traffic light waiting for a green signal, I saw a bold squirrel make its way (between cars and trucks) toward the center of the road. I winced to think about what would happen next. It was predictable, and it wasn't going to be good.

Anyone who has ever seen a squirrel in the middle of the road knows his chances of completing his journey safely are sketchy, at best. With one eye on the light and the other on the squirrel, I watched to see what would happen and breathed a sigh of relief when the squirrel completed his journey across the busy road unscathed.

How often do we take unnecessary risks like a squirrel traversing a busy road? Why? Are the lives of fellow humans not just as valuable as that of a squirrel? Being attentive to the needs of others – plants, animals, or humans – we should express care through thoughtful actions on the trail, on the road, or wherever we happen to be.

> ➤ Let your day flow like water in a stream, naturally progressing from one activity to another rather than frantically racing like a rodent.

- Create a reasonable schedule that will allow you to reach your goals.

- Forgive yourself when things don't go as you may have planned, and be grateful for other good things you've experienced or achieved.

What are some good things that have happened today that you didn't plan?

____

____

____

____

____

____

A bird's nest

Did you know... The American goldfinch uses milkweed and thistle plants for both food and construction supplies?

Next to the recreation center downtown, a small maple tree was starkly silhouetted against a whitewashed winter sky. Amid its tangled branches, I could see a small cup of grasses, sticks, and leaves that looked like a woven teacup. Countless shades of brown and gray combined with bits of now-transparent Easter grass created an earthy texture that would be impossible to duplicate.

I was beholding a one-of-a-kind piece of art – craftsmanship that might be reused by another bird, but would probably end up ravaged by harsh winds or crushed by heavy snows. It had served its purpose providing a place for eggs to be laid and baby birds to fledge. Now it was empty, a refuge that would return to the soil over time without leaving a trace.

> Consider ways to live in harmony with nature.

- Instead of buying things and throwing them away, look at either repurposing items you no longer need or giving them to an organization which can either reuse, resell, or recycle them. (See Resources.)

- If expanding or remodeling your home, explore construction materials that can minimize negative impacts on the natural world.

Write or draw what makes your home special, and you'll find it's a lot more than stuff.

____

____

____

____

Building with mud

<hr>

Mud is the oldest, most commonly used building material in the world. It has been used to build structures on every continent except for Antarctica, and in almost every climate region – from the Great Wall of China to the Taos Pueblos – for the last 7,000 years!

As a certified architect, I work with mud as a building material because generations of buildings have shown that adobe, rammed earth, cob, and wattle and daub structures are strong enough to last hundreds, if not thousands of years without succumbing to rot, termites, or fire. I use science and technology to make mud construction safer, less labor-intensive, and more accessible to each climate region and client I serve.

By contrast, 'modern' construction consumes more energy and creates more waste than any other industry in the world while thirty-year mortgages are bankrupting families with homes that will rot in 20 years.

Now, examine mud. Feel it. Squish it between your fingers. See the clay, sand, mica, and stones and try to fathom the millions of years of existence on the tips of your fingers. The DNA of your ancestors runs through this mud and into your hand as you learn how to shape and sculpt it into a built form. It's magical. It's MUD!

— April Magill, Architect, Root Down Designs

A day of rest

Did you know… The word "sabbath" is derived from "shavat," a Hebrew word meaning "to rest?"

I have spoken with people of various religious backgrounds who have told me about their sabbath – a day when they walk (rather than drive) wherever they need to go; enjoy a break from cooking, cleaning and any other kind of "work"; and most importantly, spend time worshipping something that makes a difference in their lives.

Many businesses in our town close one day each week. They do not make money on this day, but still have to pay for heat, light, and security. Is a day of rest really THAT important? I consider this question as I think about a man who works seven days each week to live his American dream. Where is his rest? Is it possible to rest in action? Looking at the natural world, one sees activity and rest simultaneously, as each plant and animal has a "shift" to gather food or rest.

> Take time each day to quietly commune with nature.

- Watch a bird fly, a squirrel dash, or a leaf flutter. Listen to the chirp of a cricket, the buzz of a cicada, or the song of a chickadee.

- Explore the practical aspects of faith that enrich daily living by making you more thoughtful, patient, and kind.

What makes faith natural? Ask a prairie that springs from the ashes of a fire more beautiful than ever. Draw or write about something that inspires you.

____

____

____

Lessons from an oak

I have always loved oak trees. Their budding spring leaves carry a gentle green that invites attention and appreciation. Their July crown, at play in the wind, sounds like thunderous applause. Fire-like autumn colors take your breath away and crinkle beneath your feet, bringing joy to young and old alike.

In contrast, winter oaks look almost dead. With cold, lifeless bark and bare limbs that seem ready to drop, they are a picture of loneliness in January's darkness. Yet without the quiet that winter brings, these trees would cease to be as beautiful as they were meant to be. Without the rest that winter brings, the deepening of roots, searching for warmth and water, oak trees could not thrive. So it is with us.

Relentless production and the absence of rest robs us of the ability to be all we are meant to be. Like the oak, we must take time to send down roots, find the center of our being, and connect with the earth.

As we walk in the woods, may we see the oaks that rise above our heads as mentors and teachers. And, may we find permission to rest. Spring and summer's beauty as well as autumn's fire will come soon enough, but for now, rest.

— Rev. Dr. Zina Jacque, Pastor, Community Church, Barrington, Illinois

Hug a tree and feel its strength

Use this page to create a bark rubbing or sketch this special tree and its location. Identify your tree using a field guide.

In the cemetery

*Did you know... The garden cemetery of the early 1900's is believed to have spawned the American park movement?**

A few years ago, I had the opportunity to visit the grave of social reformer, Jane Addams, a stately obelisk pointing heavenward. Nearby, a towering pine with huge arm-like branches stood as a silent sentinel in the little country cemetery. The pine had seen sadness and given shelter just like a friend.

When my dad passed away, he was buried in a cemetery with lots of trees, too. A gentle rain washed away mourners' tears as a great oak witnessed the arrival of yet another box to be planted in its midst. Dad worked for a school system named for "Great Oaks" so the oak tree in the cemetery was a sweet reminder of a place he loved and the strong love he abundantly shared with everyone who knew him.

Trees give cemeteries a park-like sense of welcome and timelessness that touches the heart and comforts the yearning soul. They are not frivolous or thoughtless, but an essential dimension to a place where mourning seems as intractable as soil covering a casket.

**Source: Troy Taylor, From Beyond the Grave (2000)*

> ➤ Admire trees wherever you see them.

- Quietly walk through a park or forest with a friend. Listen to the sound of your footsteps, the wind, and wildlife.

- Sit under a shady tree and look up. Admire the intricate pattern of branches overhead in the perfect order of nature.

Capture the beauty of a tree with poetry or colored pencil.

Fresh air

Thinking of fresh air makes me think of camp. One summer I worked as an environmental educator at a camp in New Jersey designed to help children from low-income communities in New York City and Patterson, New Jersey to enjoy an unforgettable summer admiring red efts, building a nature trail, picking wild blueberries, swimming in a pond bordered by bogs, and looking at stars in the dark sky above the Kittatinny Mountains. For the youth who attended this camp and those who continue to visit and return, the opportunity to have positive encounters with the natural world is priceless and irreplaceable.

Fresh air is not just essential to the body, but to the well-being of the soul. Nature is a jamboree of scents that is not like anything created by humans, or even the prettiest-smelling room deodorizer. It is the smell of rain and worms, spring lilacs, hot sun, fall leaves, and freezing air. Being outdoors distracts thought long enough to relax and renew weary humanity. It needs not promise what it already delivers.

- Go to a green space or garden in your town where you can imbibe nature's spectrum of scents, colors, textures, and sounds.

- Take a hike through a park or natural area. If such areas are too far away, try looking at the birds, mammals, trees, and plants right where you are.

- Go camping. Borrow a tent or stay in a cabin. If overnight camping is not an option, go out and look at the night sky with a local astronomy group.

- Support camping in your area – Volunteer to help at camp or donate funds for children and families needing financial aid to enjoy a fresh air experience. Contact your state's American Camping Association chapter to locate camps that will fit your needs and interests.

The ripple effect of camp

The summer of 1993 was an intense time, not long after the LA riots. I never discussed worldly events with my campers, but it seemed that they already knew too well and in ways they could not articulate, the weight of the world from living in the inner city. In spite of the challenges that faced them at home, my first and second grade campers (ages 7-9) were fun loving, vibrant children who enjoyed singing contemporary songs and giggling together.

At camp, they learned about survival in the outdoors, heard Native American stories, and participated in chores and rituals to build community. By the end of the their stay at camp, many of them learned to swim, cook, and be in nature, but most importantly make friends and have fun. This safe place provided adults that listened to them and modeled positive relationships with the environment and each other.

The program culminated with a long hike and retreat to a cabin on the opposite side of camp. It was a journey for the girls on many levels, as they were the youngest group of girls at a camp that served children in grades 1–12.

One heavy-set girl with long, straight sandy hair named Tessie cried at night because she was afraid her grandmother would die while she was at camp and that she would have no one to live with when she returned. Her mother was incarcerated and the little girl already felt responsible for her grandmother. By the end of camp, Tessie became more confident and less worried about her grandmother.

Another camper named Maddy didn't like all the rules and cried almost every night, too. Terrified by the sound of the crickets and fearful of animals in the forest, she didn't stop crying until the last few nights of camp. Years later, she became a counselor at the same camp when she was in college.

It was a summer that changed my life, too. Over the years, I have not forgotten the songs I sang with my fellow counselors to help the girls sleep or the beautiful bear and her cubs that visited our outdoor kitchen when we forgot to take out the compost. After working at camp, I became interested in the study of resiliency and restorative justice that evolved from Indigenous peoples' circles of community and conflict resolution. This led to a career in the arts advocacy, community outreach, and social services.

— Esperanza Altamar, Artist & Social Services Case Manager, Buffalo, NY

Joie de vivre

Did you know… "Joie de vivre" is French for "joy of life"?

What makes you happy? Close your eyes, take a deep breath, and visit a place in time where you felt the warmth of a sunbeam, the caress of a gentle breeze, or the beauty of a sky so blue it made your heart flutter like a passing songbird.

Open your eyes to the nature of today. Even though you may not be in a beautiful outdoor setting nor have a window in your office, you can hold onto the joy you've experienced while sharing it with others.

- If love is at the heart of everything you do, happiness is only natural.

- Smile. It is hard not to be happy when your face is smiling.

- Volunteer! Help others in your community or take a volunteer vacation where you can help people in other parts of the country or world using your special talents.

- Do something good for neighbors, friends or coworkers. Give a call, bring a treat, or share a positive thought. Your very presence can bring joy!

Joy isn't just an emotion that comes forth when things are going well. Joy is the kingdom of Light springing up from within you as the child of Light. It is the power to feel alive, which enables you to say "I love being alive." Joy flows from Love. It is like the sun and its rays. We are the shining forth the rays of Love's joy.

Reaching out to give love to someone such as going to a neighbor to give them a hug or even a loving phone call can restore joy in your heart. Living caring love is a joy to our heart and to the one receiving it. It is a sense of the very presence of divine Love.

One sunny winter day as I was picking up children I took to Sunday School, I noticed their grandmother was in tears. She didn't feel well and was frustrated that the children weren't ready. As I acknowledged the power of Love, the children quieted down and got ready quickly while their grandmother found a sense of peace. Love changed the room to Light and joy. Love's joy helped to establish a sense of harmony at Sunday School, and wellness for a grandmother. Joy brings victory.

— Sondra Nielsen Elkins, Cincinnati, OH

Richness

"The one who dies with the most toys wins," boasted a bumper sticker on a car in front of me. Cars, trucks, motorcycles, boats, RVs, TVs, and SUVs are just part of the alphabet soup that would appear to make a person rich.

Do the latest "toys" make you rich or simply fill other voids in your life?

If richness is about living in a way that recognizes the goodness already present, perhaps one should focus on incorporating more naturally expansive spiritual qualities into daily living.

- ➢ Live abundantly.

- Discover the richness in your life – the beauty of a sunrise, the song of a bird, or the sweet scent of a flower – and express this joy with a smile, a kind note, or a simple word.

- Find something to be thankful for when the weather is dismal, no one calls, or things don't go as planned.

Record what makes you happy – friends, family, co-workers, home, special places.

____

____

____

____

____

____

It is so easy to become caught up in the mundane aspects of life. But life is not just a round of chores and work. Think about where you place your attention and energy. The night sky is full of starry wonder. Think about the infinite possibilities of your own potential. If something intrigues you or draws your attention, explore that interest. Be more aware of the many beautiful sensations and delights of sight, sound, taste, touch, and scent that each day brings. It may lead you to a whole new adventure. This is where true wisdom and lasting richness lives.

— Candy Paull, Author of *The Heart of Abundance*

Secondhand

When I think about shopping, I cringe. Everything seems so expensive!

Do I really need this new thing or that? Some things I cannot avoid purchasing, but many items, I can. Styles change constantly. Old and new switch places as quickly as partners at a square dance.

What is the value of buying something used? In some cases, it's extreme savings. Though not one to advocate buying junk, I like to shop at secondhand stores and support community thrift shops because they keep a lot of stuff out of landfills and provide funding to worthy organizations or local "green" entrepreneurs.

- ➤ Consider buying secondhand merchandise.

- Ask friends, family members and neighbors or join an online service to find people who want to get rid of the things you'd like to acquire.

- Consider sharing. We expect children to do it; so, why not adults?

- Do you really need to have your own tent or could you purchase one with a friend and take turns using it?

- Look at what you have. Can you repair a broken item or does it need to be replaced? What other alternatives exist? Look in the phone book for local repair shops or resale/thrift stores.

What are you planning to buy within the next day? Week? Month? Year? Why? List ways to share the cost and benefits with your family and friends.

____

____

____

____

____

____

____

The road less traveled

Two roads diverged in a wood, and I—
I took the one less traveled by,
And that has made all the difference.

— Robert Frost

There is something primitive about dirt roads. Travel on a dirt road when it's dry, and you can taste dust. Go out after a storm and the scents of earth mingle with reflections of sky in intermittent puddles bordered by dark, sticky mud.

I didn't grow up in the country, nor do I live there now, but I still feel a strong connection to dirt roads.

When I worked at camp, dirt roads connected all of the units together within camp, and beyond. Laden with potholes, ruts, dust, and mud, the roads were often blanketed with gravel to keep them navigable throughout the year.

From Illinois State Route 47, some of these roads still peel off into farms, providing a place for tractors and horses to travel undisturbed, even as suburbia swallows more farmland.

While dirt roads are not designed for fast travel, you should try experiencing them on foot, horseback, bike, tractor, or pickup truck. Such rustic and rutted dirt roads allow us to escape civilization and return to simpler times.

> ➤ Put your imagination to work: Travel back in time

- Visit a camp or natural area with dirt roads or paths. Carefully walk or bike on the dirt road or path and look around. Dirt roads are most enjoyable and least damaged when they are not muddy.

- What would earlier people have seen, heard, or experienced? What remains the same?

Record your thoughts.

____

____

____

____

____

Forgiveness

*Did you know… Some research suggests forgiveness may bolster the immune system, lower blood pressure, reduce depression and increase longevity?**

If you've ever made a mistake or been wronged in some way, you have grappled with forgiveness. Will I be forgiven? Should I forgive another? A nearby church once posted "forgiveness is the sweetest revenge," making me think about the topic as I went about my day. Is forgiveness really part of our nature?

Forgiveness does not mean that a wrongdoer goes unpunished or that the one who has been hurt needs to be hurt again. It simply means that the person who has been hurt doesn't retain resentment.

In the natural world, soil forgives us for removing plants by covering itself with weeds. In order to restore land to its native beauty, it must receive special care.

- Let restoration work inspire you to forgive yourself and others for past wrongs.

- Work on a local native landscape restoration project – remove a weed or invasive tree, and plant a native seed or tree. Revisit the area that is sown with love and behold its beauty.

- Observe how natural areas recover from storms and other catastrophic events. Forgiveness is natural, sending down roots and blooming in the hearts of those who are strong enough to look beyond tragedy to the promising sunlight of hope..

**Source: Mayo Clinic, Johns Hopkins Medicine*

How does restoration work make you feel?

____

____

____

____

____

____

Save the soil

*Did you know…"Soil erosion is the #1 source of pollution to surface water in Maine?"**

Old boat ramps, dirt roads, and ditches lacking vegetation to slow the flow of water, lose soil during heavy rains.

Far from Maine, I see it where I live, as chocolaty brown water enters the river during a heavy rain. Bits of soil creep down slopes into waterways leaving deep trenches in their wake. From there, they coat the bottom of rocky streams with a layer of silt which destroys habitat for many aquatic creatures.

> ➢ Protect the soil in your community.

- Stay on designated trails. Winding trails with switchbacks are designed to minimize erosion.

- Whenever possible, map and report erosion problems to your village board, water resources department, state EPA, or Army Corps of Engineers.

- Cover exposed soil with something biodegradable (like coconut fiber) until you can get some vegetative cover established. Select native plants adapted to the conditions in your yard.

**Source: Maine Department of Environmental Protection, Bureau of Land & Water Quality*

On the next page, keep a list of native plants that grow best in your area and look for places to purchase them. For more information, visit your state's department of natural resources, USEPA, and National Wildlife Federation in addition to Wild Ones Native Plants, Natural Landscapes.

The immense root systems of native plants, especially graminoid grasses and sedges, absorb rain, thereby preventing runoff, erosion, and flooding. One garden won't save the world – but a subdivision of native plants will do some good.

— Patricia Hill, Native Landscape Designer & Author of *Design your own Midwest Garden*

Touch a rock

Do something that puts your hands and/or feet in touch with rocks or sand and share your experience.

Date: _______________________________

Location: _______________________________

Temp/weather: _______________________________

Rocks

Did you know... Fossils may be found in some areas without digging? Wherever there is sedimentary rock, there is an opportunity to discover fossils!

Growing up in an unglaciated area with plenty of rocky creeks, I enjoyed hunting for marine fossils that were older than dinosaurs.

While I could not begin to fathom 450 million years (the approximate age of these fossils), I could appreciate the amazingly preserved features of a tiny crinoid section (nicknamed a fairy ring) and a smaller than pinky-sized *zygospira modesta* shell.

Some fossilized shells resemble those found in oceans and rivers today. Much like today, some shells were pulverized by strong currents while others got stuck in the mud, leaving a few perfect specimens for the meticulous fossil hunter.

I was introduced to this hobby by my mom, an amateur paleontologist who used her knowledge to inspire countless school children to look beneath their feet.

> Look beneath your feet.

- If you live in an area impacted by glaciers, you will probably not find fossils, but an amazing variety of colorful rocks from faraway places. If you reside in a place where volcanoes have shaped the landscape, you will have find other treasures. Learn about the rocks where you live.

- Explore the world from more than your current vantage point. Look at something from a different perspective or visit another place.

- Appreciate something you discover and its role in the universe.

Write about the underlying purpose of something that inspires you today.

____

____

____

____

____

____

On being a river gene carrier

Looking at all the ways my life has been woven with water, I can't help but believe that I carry a "river gene." My father enjoyed childhood adventures around the Delaware River, and his grandfather was a fisherman there.

While I didn't have much experience with rivers as a child in the 1950's, I couldn't resist walking on (and falling off) slippery, partially submerged logs in a pond near my bus stop. When I was child, my family spent a week at a lake in Michigan where my dad taught me to canoe. It wasn't until college that I signed up for a canoe trip.

My canoe partner Zelda, who was quite experienced, skillfully handled the stern. Near the end of the trip, I asked to switch places. Within minutes, I had us moving sideways into an obstacle, which resulted in an embarrassing swim in a cold creek. Two years later, I landed a summer job at a School Forest in central Wisconsin where I volunteered to be the canoeing instructor. I learned by doing, and became pretty proficient.

In 1982, a friend offered me a position as a raft guide near Yellowstone that turned into an eighteen year career, and led to adopting whitewater kayaking as a favorite activity. When I was not working as a raft guide, I taught high school science and integrated canoeing into the curriculum of several courses.

Nine years later, I became an educator for Friends of the Fox River. Only a few states had citizen scientist programs at the time and I was excited about spearheading our flagship Watershed Watchdog program, enabling thousands of people to learn how to protect water quality. This was a turning point for me as a teacher. I had found a niche that both excited me, and was an incredible vehicle for many facets of the educational experience.

Getting students into the Fox River to collect water quality data continues to be magical, as each student finds a comfortable sense of place. My gradual exposure to rivers throughout my life has provided views and tools that now inspire me to work everyday to connect others with local streams through environmental literacy and stewardship to enhance water quality.

The river fills my soul, and carries my spirit. I carry a river gene, and so do you.

— Gary Swick, President, Friends of the Fox River

Another reason to go creeking

*Did you know... The Fox River drains 2,658 square miles of land in southern Wisconsin and northern Illinois?**

I have always liked creeking. It all began when I was a child growing up in southern Ohio. My mom took me fossil hunting in seemingly endless winding paths of rock and water at nearby parks.

Where did these creeks begin? Where did they end? What happened along the way? I never knew.

As an adult, I would eventually spend time on the Rock River leading water quality monitoring workshops and volunteering on the Fox River with a local preservation group to gather data to help monitor a watershed. It was fun to have an excuse to go creeking again.

- Try monitoring the water quality where you live.

- Explore ways to retain and filter water where you live using rain garden and wetland plantings.

- Limit the use of chemicals on your lawn and in your household.

- Contact your local waste collector to find out about hazardous waste and medicine disposal.

- Join a local river or stream monitoring group, get trained, and gather data. Look at trends in your data and see what can be done to improve water quality.

**Source: Fox River Study Group*

Draw a picture of your favorite creek. Describe how it makes you feel in a few words.

Catch the rain

*Did you know... Using a rain barrel can save 1300 gallons of water during peak summer months? A full rain barrel can provide enough water to give a 240 square foot garden over 1/3" of water!**

Last year I purchased my first rain barrel and have been amazed at the dividends. While I don't drink the water that comes off the roof, I have found it to be great for watering plants, washing mud-covered hands, cleaning the birdbath, and washing the car. By keeping this water in a barrel, I reduce runoff, and lower the water bill. I keep a resource more precious than oil, rationed by some communities during droughts, conveniently next to my house.

> ➤ Be grateful for rain by using what you receive.

- Install barrels beneath downspouts near to your gardens.

- Create a rain garden using deeply rooted native wildflowers to filter water and keep it local.

**Source: University of Florida, Miami – Dade Extension Service*

I teach others about water conservation by example. At home, I have two rain barrels and a rain garden. The rain barrel provides rainwater for my pets while a rain garden offers habitat for native wildflowers and their pollinators.

Rainwater is different from the City tap water where I live because it does not have all of the chemicals used to sanitize it for human consumption. Both Cassie and Cali have water bowls filled with chlorinated tap water in the kitchen, but prefer drinking rainwater from a bowl I keep in front of the backyard rain barrel.

I can see the difference in the plants that I water with the rainwater versus the garden hose, too. The plants that get rainwater are fuller and larger than the ones I water with tap water. Plants prefer rain with minerals that are naturally soft. My best rain garden is one that I made where my air conditioner drains. The hotter it is, the more the air conditioner runs causing the condensation drain to keep the garden moist during droughts. If it's raining, a downspout directed to the same garden enables it to be irrigated by water that would have become runoff. Marsh marigold and great blue lobelia are some of the flowers that adorn this backyard habitat.

— Jim Kleinwachter, Land Preservation Specialist and Conservation@ Home Founder, The Conservation Foundation

Sketch

Sketch the layout of your home, its downspouts, and locations where it would make sense to gather water or create a rain garden.

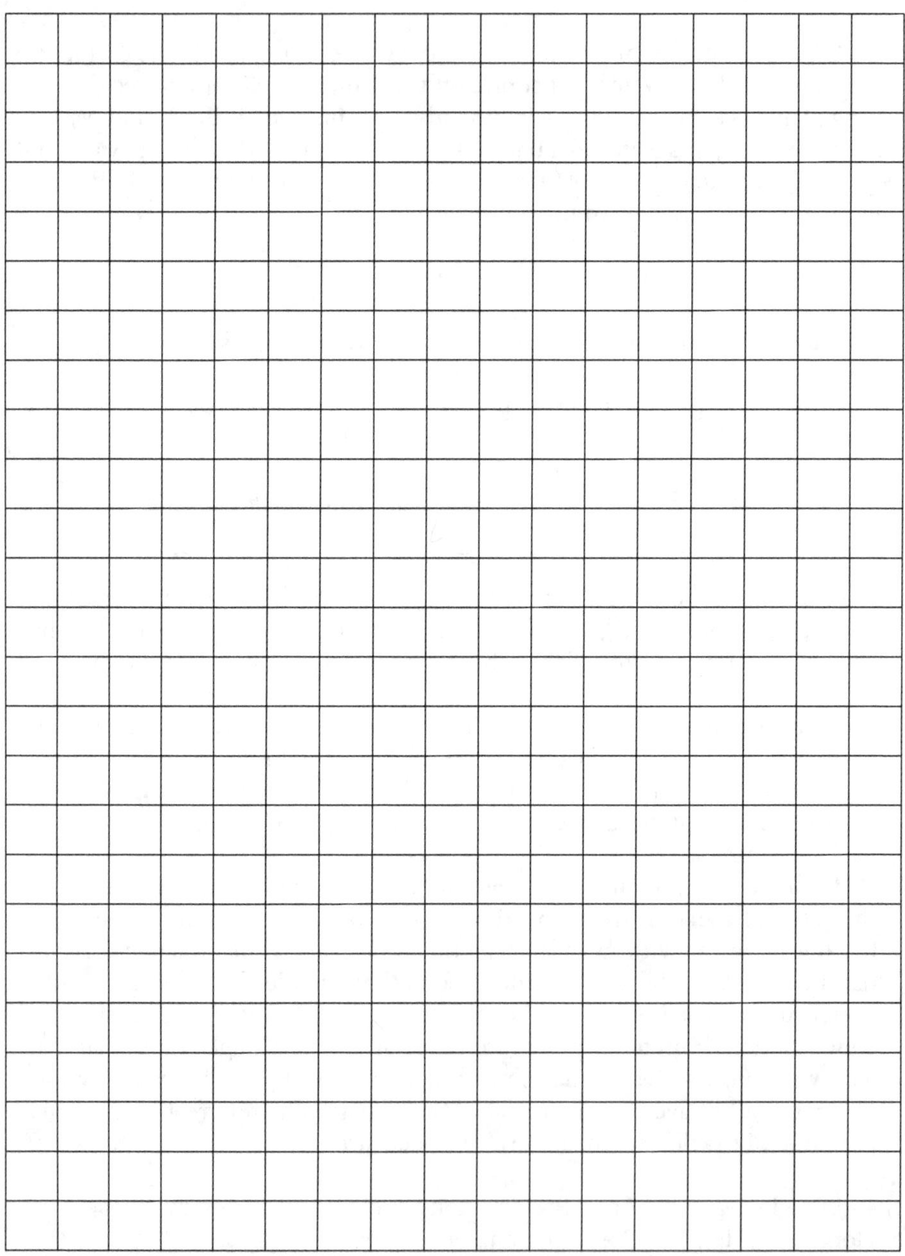

The grass is always greener

Did you know… Lawns cover over 50,000 square miles of American soil? About 20,000 miles of turf are treated with herbicide and pesticide.

Historically, homes with modest yards like ours were landscaped with packed dirt, herbs, flowers, and vegetables, while turf-covered lawns were reserved for more expansive estates. By the late 18th century, weed-free lawns became the fashion, followed by mechanical mowers in 1885.

Our neighbor, a meticulous retired gentleman, is king of the green. I have never seen anyone dote over a lawn the way this man does – religiously mowing, edging, weeding by hand, and treating it with chemicals to add to its overall lushness. The sound of his mower sends guilt through the hearts of his immediate neighbors who begrudgingly follow suit, until the entire block looks like one plush green carpet of uniform vegetation.

Unfortunately, thirty minutes of mowing produces as much pollution as a car driving 172 miles.* Electric mowers reduce carbon dioxide emissions by 99.9% but need to be plugged in or charged. Old-fashioned push mowers require more stamina and more frequent mowing. Wouldn't it be better to have less grass?

**Source: California Air Resources Board*

> ➤ Look at ways to use native plants, grasses, and landscaping elements to decrease the need for conventional turf, and subsequent mowing.

- Consider replacing part of your lawn with low maintenance native plants.

- Pull, cover or spot kill weeds whenever possible to minimize chemical runoff.

Caring for nature enriches community

When Linda and I moved to Northbrook twenty years ago, I wanted to create native wildflowers beds in our yard to raise seed for conservation. I contacted the Village to see if there were any ordinances to consider and discussed the idea with our new neighbors. Everyone was either okay with it or positively tickled by the concept. I worked hard to keep the yard well-behaved, flowery, and butterfly-filled.

In the decades since, many neighbors have asked us for advice and started including native plantings in their own yards. Their children have raised monarch butterflies from the eggs found on the milkweeds in our little nature patches, while forest preserve districts have used seeds from some of our more rare plants to restore natural ecosystems. One neighbor, Heeyoung Kim, became an internationally recognized illustrator of rare plants, starting with the ones she fell in love with in our yard.

This wild yard is like a member of the family, sometimes demanding, but always enriching our lives.

— Stephen Packard, Conservationist

Create a sketch of your yard. Mark areas where grass is not flourishing or might be readily replaced by other vegetation.

A tree for woodpecker

Did you know... Downy woodpeckers breed and nest in the summer? Others begin their nests in spring, while squirrels construct their leafy winter nests in fall. Removing dead trees during these seasons should only be done if there a safety hazard to humans. Special care should be taken to prevent any animals from losing their home.

Next to a pond at a nearby natural area stands a somewhat gangly black willow tree that has a trunk branching in three directions. As volunteers were clearing the area around it to make room for native habitat, I pondered its purpose. It didn't possess conventional landscape beauty, and it wasn't behaving like an invasive, so I asked the volunteers to leave it, not knowing why.

A few weeks later, I stood on the dock with a group of children and their teachers admiring the pond when I discovered the reason for saving the tree. In one of its hollow lower branches lived a dainty downy woodpecker. I had seen the holes, but now saw a small black-and-white feathered resident. Even "not-so-pretty" trees and shrubs serve a purpose in the natural community.

- Provide habitat for wildlife in your own yard.

- When possible, leave dead trees standing for insects and birds.

- If there are trees or plants that threaten your health or safety, have them removed, then replace them with native flower, fruit, and/or nut-bearing plants, shrubs, or trees.

- Avoid removing trees or shrubs during nesting season.

The value of oaks

The value of oaks for supporting both vertebrate and invertebrate wildlife cannot be overstated – 557 species of *Lepidoptera* alone depend on oak trees!

Since the demise of the American chestnut, oaks have joined hickories, walnuts, and the American beech in supplying the bulk of nut forage so necessary for maintaining populations of vertebrate wildlife. Acorns fill the bellies of deer, raccoons, turkeys, mice, black bear, squirrels, and even wood ducks. Cavities that develop in living and dead oak giants supply vital nesting sites for dozens of species of birds including chickadees, wrens, downy and hairy woodpeckers, flickers, owls, and bluebirds.

All species have the potential to sink or save an ecosystem, depending on the circumstances. Restoring large stands of oaks to suburbia would go a long way toward shoring up the future of our nation's biodiversity. Biodiversity is essential to the stability – indeed, the very existence – of most ecosystems. We can make a measurable difference almost immediately by planting a native nearby.

— Douglas Tallamy, Entomologist and Author of *Bringing Nature Home: How You can sustain Wildlife with Native Plants*

Here kitty, kitty...

*Did you know... About 50% of American cats live indoors? Another 70 million feral and stray cats roam the streets and countryside.**

When I was a child, my mom used to feed our neighbor's cat and give him a bowl of milk now and then. Other cats gradually learned about the doorstep offerings and showed up, too. Mom was careful to take the food inside at night, but the situation persisted until we moved.

If you see a cat roaming around your neighborhood, ask your neighbors about it. Does it have a home or is it wild? If it has a home, it needs to stay there. Cats eat songbirds, chipmunks and other small animals that provide food for owls, raccoons, and other wildlife. Leaving cats outside for extended periods of time disrupts nature's balance.

> ➤ Protect wildlife and pets.

- Stay with and monitor the activities of your cat, dog, or other animals when they go outside.

- If you encounter a cat that is feral, try to set a live trap for it and contact animal control for assistance. Never handle a wild cat or kitten.

- Contact your local chapter of the Society for the Prevention of Cruelty to Animals (SPCA) and see what you can do to educate others about feral cat colonies.

**Source: National Geographic News 2004*

What impact does your cat or other pet have on the natural world? Brainstorm ways you can protect your pet and promote natural balance in your ecological community.

____

____

____

____

____

A dead raccoon on the road of life

Driving down the road, I saw a dead raccoon lying across the double yellow line. Dawn outlined its crumpled body atop the inhospitable asphalt. I silently mourned, wondering about the pain and final sorrow-filled moments of this pitiful creature, a risk-taker who paid the ultimate price, becoming frozen in time and space.

What can we do to prevent accidents, help injured wildlife and improve our natural surroundings?

- ➢ Be alert.

- Driving does not make you the "king of the road", but increases your responsibility as a steward for the natural world.

- Slow down in natural and rural areas. Tractors and shifting herds of livestock have their own sense of time. Cultivate patience.

- Watch for wildlife at the edge of roads (especially around dawn and dusk). Where one animal travels, others are likely to follow.

- Find local wildlife rehabilitators online or through your town's animal control person BEFORE you're faced with a challenge of this nature.

Create a list of local wildlife rehabilitators.

Birds: ____

____

Mammals: ____

____

Reptiles: ____

____

Amphibians: ____

____

Other: ____

A snake in the parking lot

Did you know… In a 1946 report titled "Reptiles and Amphibians" by Yosemite National Park's Associate Park Naturalist Myrl V. Walker, "the most recent and perhaps the most devastating enemy of the snake is the automobile"?

While we were on vacation at a national park, we saw a snake in the parking lot. It was a small snake, but a real spectacle. I took a picture, so I could identify it. Other tourists followed suit. The rangers eventually had to shoo curious tourists away from the heat-loving reptile, which had chosen to bask on the asphalt over waiting for the sun to warm its natural habitat.

As a tour bus pulled out of the lot, my son cried, "I think the bus ran over it." Not wanting to see a lifeless body on the asphalt, I looked away quickly, but had to turn back. The snake was gone without a trace. It had escaped back into the mowed grass in front of the nature center, escaping what seemed a most certain demise.

- Stop, look, and enjoy wildlife wherever you are.

- Admire plants and animals everywhere you go – not just in the woods.

- When you find a plant or animal outside its typical habitat, try to understand why.

- Share your discoveries with caring conservation colleagues.

From little acorns grow mighty oaks

*Did you know… Only 6% of American children ages 9-13 play outside?**

When my children were young, I visited a preschool for 3- and 4-year-olds at the local high school. It was a led by two groups of female high school students aspiring to be preschool teachers.

Outnumbered by their caregivers, the small group of children seemed well adjusted and well behaved. One child played at the popcorn table the entire time he was given free time. The high school students took turns playing next to him, but their interactions were minimal. Other children found their niches elsewhere and played in their parallel universes until the bell was rung, transitioning them to group music, snack, and craft activities.

The lead teacher explained the importance of play, but in the same breath said that the children would not be able to go outside, as they had lost their outdoor play space. My heart sank. For some of these children, this might be their only opportunity to play outdoors. Without positive experiences in nature, these children might not be inclined to spend time outdoors nor value the natural world as adults.

➢ Facilitate positive encounters with nature.

- Spend at least 5 minutes every day outdoors, not just reading the paper or playing a sport, but taking a walk or watching a bird build a nest.

- Encourage neighboring families to spend time in nature, too.

- Volunteer to help children get outdoors at local schools. Provide assistance to start a school-based garden or outdoor learning area.

**Source: National Wildlife Federation*

Write about how connecting with the natural world or watching children relate to the natural world has inspired you. Brainstorm other ways to get kids outdoors.

Why reconnect with nature?

Time in nature is not leisure time; it's an essential investment in our children's health (and also, by the way, in our own).

As a boy, I was unaware that my woods were ecologically connected with any other forests. Nobody in the 1950s talked about acid rain or holes in the ozone layer or global warming. But I knew my woods and my fields; I knew every bend in the creek and dip in the beaten dirt paths. I wandered those woods even in my dreams. A kid today can likely tell you about the Amazon rain forest—but not about the last time he or she explored the woods in solitude, or lay in a field listening to the wind and watching the clouds move.

...Healing the broken bond between our young and nature—is in our self-interest, not only because aesthetics or justice demands it, but also because our mental, physical, and spiritual health depends upon it. The health of the earth is at stake as well.

— Richard Louv, Author of *Last Child in the Woods: Saving our Children from Nature Deficit Disorder*

Do you talk to plants?

Growing up in northern Illinois with a plant-filled "sun parlor" was the beginning of a journey that led to a lifelong hobby and career in interior landscaping. For over 30 years, I owned and operated a company that used plants to enhance corporate lobbies, offices, banks, and restaurants to present an image of well-being, prosperity, and hospitality.

People would form a bond (often unrecognized and unconscious) with "their" office plant. Certainly we do this with plants at home, making them quasi family-members.

With watering can in hand, I became an ambassador, educator, and researcher because people were curious. Noticing what I was doing, they would offer opinions and stories. They would even ask questions about what was going on with their plants at home, as though I would be able to somehow "divine" the answer sight unseen! In many cases, I could offer a "gentle nudge" to hasten the end of a suffering plant.

"Do you talk to plants?" some people ask. "Not out loud," I say, as communicating with plants requires using a different "frequency". Putting myself in their place, I assess their present state against what would be optimal and look for clues in the condition of soil and leaves.

Working with interior landscaping, has inspired me to learn about landscaping beyond the door and begin restoring native species to the degraded farmland that is my yard. All living things are connected, and should be respected and sustained by each other. Plants do this for us. Do we do this for them?

— Jean Muntz, Perpetually Evolving Gardener

Living on the edge (of my window sill)

Did you know... Early Greeks and Romans cultivated indoor gardens.

If houseplants sound like an oxymoron, then it's time to look at the value of having something green in your abode. Plants reduce noise by absorbing and reflecting sound, and improve air quality by absorbing toxins and providing oxygen. They add beauty and color amid the drear of winter and contribute to a home-like atmosphere.

> ➢ Embrace the beauty of nature inside and out.

- Assess your needs before you acquire any plants. Do you have time to water and transplant or are you looking for something that will grow slowly with little attention?

- Look at your space and sunlight situation, so you can choose a plant that will thrive.

- Check the safety of your "favorites" if pets or children are present.

- Consider plants that are practical (such as aloe vera, cooking herbs, and plants that improve air quality).

- Let your friends know you're interested in cultivating houseplants and see if you can get some seedlings from their plants.

Look at the qualities that make your houseplant perfect for your home and consider how these qualities are valuable in other parts of your life. Some qualities to consider might include resilience, low maintenance beauty, and steady growth.

____

____

____

____

____

____

One less flush

Did you know... Toilets built before 1982 use about 5-7 gallons of water per flush? Today's toilets average about 1.6 gallons per flush.

This may sound gross, but our family rarely flushes the toilet after everyone goes to bed. Unless there is poop or someone is feeling ill, we leave the flushing until morning, saving about 4-5 flushes per night – nearly 8 gallons of water per day! Saving water saves money and conserves water. Modern two flush toilets (low flow for urine and higher flow for excrement) and gray water systems (which reuse water from bathroom sinks and tubs) are making tremendous strides in conservation.

Since 3% percent of the earth's water is freshwater (and 68.7% of this is tied up in glaciers and ice caps!), freshwater is a valuable commodity.*

- Consider ways to conserve water in your home.

- Don't use the toilet to get rid of things that can be disposed of in other ways (like used tissues).

- Install a toilet dam, plastic displacement bag or a milk jug full of gravel, so less water will be used when the toilet is flushed. Do NOT use a brick, as bricks can disintegrate and lead to other toilet troubles.

- If your toilet needs to be replaced, consider an ultra-low or low flush model. Always listen for running water and check for leaks.

**Source: U.S. Geological Survey*

List other ways you can conserve water in your home.

____

____

____

____

____

____

Saving water (without taking a shorter shower)

My best friend Lois used to live in Santa Fe, NM, where water is scarcer and more costly than it is in Chicago. When I visited her, I noticed that she kept a bucket in her shower stall. Every morning while she waited for the water to warm up, she captured that water in her bucket and used it to water her plants and garden. It's perfectly good drinking water going down the drain. (If you live in an apartment, you can use the water to flush your toilet or fill your pet's water bowl.) So I started doing this as well, and discovered that I am capturing 10-15 gallons per week in that minute or less it takes for the shower to warm up. The cost savings is pennies, but it's another small thing I can do to conserve water and demonstrate good stewardship. (Note: Not all showers are designed to have water flow from a faucet or tap fixture first, so you may not be able to do this in your home.)

— Debra Shore, Chicago Metropolitan Water Reclamation District Commissioner

Hydrocarbons, nitrogen oxides and carbon monoxide, oh my!

*Did you know... Transportation is the #1 contributor to air pollution in the U.S.**

While I enjoyed visiting California as a child, the appearance of thick brown smog in the sky over Los Angeles made me feel sad. Bumper-to-bumper traffic combined with geography and weather continue to undermine the health of this beautiful landscape and its inhabitants.

Vehicle regulations have reduced what are "acceptable levels" of emissions for each vehicle on the road, but more Americans are behind the wheel than ever. As strides are being made to improve air quality in Los Angeles and other major cities, we must investigate ways we can actively nurture recovery.

- Explore other ways to get where you want to go.

- Combine errands. If you must drive, park the car in one place and walk.

- Carpool or use public transportation to reduce traffic and enjoy others.

- Use a vehicle that doesn't require fossil fuels, like an electric car or bicycle.

**Source: Union of Concerned Scientists, 2004*

Over our lifetimes, we are witnessing profound changes in our climate systems. Our actions are responsible for a substantial part of the climate changes we've observed. We can see the impacts of human-caused climate change on many things that have value for us – glaciers and coral reefs, plants and animals, human health and water availability.

Learn about climate science. Understand the scientific evidence telling us that human actions are affecting global climate and the likely climate outcomes if we don't address this problem. Without scientifically savvy citizens, we won't be able to make informed decisions on how to respond to the problem of human-caused climate change. Climate change isn't just a scientific problem to be studied with computer models and observations. In the end, it's fundamentally a moral and ethical problem, a question all of us must face: What kind of world do we want to leave behind for future generations?

— Dr. Benjamin Santer, Atmospheric Scientist, Lawrence Livermore National Lab

Try bicycling

Did you know... In 2010, there were 140 Bicycle Friendly Communities in the U.S.

When I was growing up, I used to ride on the hilly roads from my home to the home of a friend about a mile away. There was little, if any berm, and many areas where drivers could not see the road ahead. I never worried about being hit by a car because I was young and in my mind, invincible.

I continue to ride today, but not with the carefree spirit I once embodied. Inattentive cell phone users, individuals expressing road rage, and hasty egotists threaten peaceful passage.

Well-planned bike lanes or trails to connect people to shopping, schools, or natural areas are still needed. Narrow sidewalks line some busy roads, but such alternatives are not ideal when pedestrians are present. Bicycles can reach speeds comparable to a car. For bicycle-based transportation to be more widely adopted, more people have to feel safe.

Source: The League of American Bicyclists

> - Support bicycling in your community.

- Accept cyclists as fellow travelers and share the road with them as you would with any other vehicle.

- Learn bicycling hand signals and etiquette (riding with traffic and obeying traffic signals) whether you choose to ride or not.

- Encourage your city and county road commissioners to provide space for cyclists to ride – including multi-use trails and roadway paths.

- Wear a helmet, bring a cell phone, carry water and snacks, and keep identification with you on all rides.

Let there be light

Did you know... A 75-watt incandescent light bulb produces as much light as an 18-watt compact fluorescent one.

I wake up early and turn on a light to see what I'm doing. Just after sunrise, I begin to open the curtains and gradually turn off the artificial lights. Natural light fills each room with ample light for completing chores and eating meals, but needs to supplemented in my office and other dark places on a regular basis.

Using sunlight instead of artificial lighting not only saves money, but acknowledges the peaceful beauty nature brings to daily life.

> ➢ Use natural light.

- Work by windows and/or skylights as much as possible.

- Replace incandescent bulbs with compact fluorescent bulbs, which last up to 10 times longer and use about 1/4 of the energy.

- Turn off the light when you leave a room.

Analyze your consumption of light at home, work, and school. Look for places where you can switch all or half of the lights off on a sunny day.

____

____

____

____

____

____

____

____

Let there be darkness

*Did you know... At least 30% of all outdoor lighting in the US goes directly into the night sky via unshielded outdoor lights?**

Like birds, moths, frogs, and so many other creatures, I have always been drawn to the spectacle of light – floodlights, holiday lights, architectural lights, etc. I cannot lie about my affair with light. I was taught to fear darkness and to make sure I always left a light glowing in the window.

While artificial night lighting can be handy, criminals favor highly lit facades because they can lurk in shadows, see dogs, and get a clearer view of what they want to steal.

Artificial night lighting which is not correctly placed causes light pollution, and impacts the well-being of plants, animals, and people! Worst of all, it deprives children of the opportunity to find a star to make a wish.

➢ Minimize the use of artificial night light whenever possible

- Close the curtains at sunset to keep light in the house (especially during spring and fall migration), as birds are more likely to fly into windows during these times of year.

- Set up motion sensors or timers to turn off lights inside and out.

- If you must use lights outdoors, add red or yellow filters to energy-efficient lights. Red lights have less impact on wildlife and yellow lights such as high pressure sodium (HPS) or low pressure sodium (LPS) attract fewer insects and moths. Install fully shielded or full cutoff fixtures to direct outdoor lighting to where it is needed most – on the ground.

**Source: International Dark-Sky Association*

Look at the night sky and write about your feelings

____

____

____

____

____

Hot and cold

*Did you know... Office workers tend to be most productive in facilities with temperatures heated or cooled to 72°F?**

During the summer, I frequently feel uncomfortably cold indoors. I like the idea of being cool, but often end up in restaurants, stores, or other public areas where the air conditioning blows straight on my back or arms and sends my poorly insulated body into goosebumps and shivers. While heating and cooling has its place, common sense and balance should prevail.

In the natural world, pigs wallow in mud puddles, deer don lighter coats of fur, and birds migrate to climates that suit their needs. We, too, should welcome summer as a season of abundance and growth in spite of increased heat and bugs, putting away winter clothing, swimming with friends, and visiting cooler areas much like our animal counterparts.

> ➤ Consciously adapt to the climate where you live.

- In summer, seek naturally cooler places in your home or community. Take advantage of fans and breezes whenever possible.

- For winter, keep the thermostat as low as you can comfortably leave it.

- Wear clothes appropriate to the season – sweaters, wool socks and thick pants to keep warm, and lighter clothes in warmer weather.

- Recreate outdoors – bike in spring, swim in summer, hike in fall, ski in winter to get warmer or cooler.

**Source: Effect of Office Temperature on Task Performance in Office Environment (Seppanen, Fisk, Lei 2006)*

What can you do to be more comfortable with the climate where you live?

____

____

____

____

____

More than cores and crusts

Did you know… An average American family throws away approximately 25% of the food and beverages they buy – that's about $1,365 – $2,275 per year for a family of four?

My mom always used to say, "waste not, want not," insisting that we eat everything we put on our plates. Call it accountability, but she grew up during The Great Depression and abhorred waste of any kind.

One outdoor education center where I worked required children to weigh and record the amount of food they threw away after each meal. At the end of their stay, the table of students with the least amount of waste received a prize. Competition was fierce, as students encouraged their classmates to be more mindful consumers by taking only what they were going to eat.

Today, some people try to point out the wastefulness of Americans by getting their sustenance from dumpsters. Others have begun food recovery programs in schools to provide good food for those in need before it ever reaches a dumpster or landfill.

➢ Reduce your waste.

- Make a menu and stick to it, especially when it comes to using fresh fruits and vegetables.

- Consider composting food and plant waste – hot composting (with a pile or bin) or vermicomposting (with worms).

- Gather unopened prepackaged food at work or school to feed the hungry.

**Source: American Wasteland, Jonathon Bloom. Wasted: How America Is Losing Up to 40 Percent of Its Food from Farm to Fork to Landfill, Dana Gunders, Natural Resources Defense Council*

Create a plan for composting where you live, work, go to school.

____

____

____

____

Anyone can compost

Did you know... Organic material – food scraps, yard trimmings, untreated wood, paper and paperboard – is the largest single component of our garbage in the US?

If we allow nature's systems to do their work, we can save money and help the environment. Our soil will be healthier, and our water will be cleaner.

Compost harnesses nutrients and water from food scraps and puts them back into soil. It's a great natural fertilizer, retaining water, reducing soil erosion, and decreasing the need for chemical fertilizers. Compost keeps organic materials out of landfills and reduces methane (greenhouse gas) emissions.

Anyone can compost. If you have a yard, you can compost in your yard. If you don't, you can compost indoors with worms. From curbside programs in big cities to small-scale businesses, composting invites us to participate in a system of waste management that has proven its value for millions of years.

– Kay McKeen, Founder & Executive Director, SCARCE

Unwrapping resources

Did you know… Each year, an average American generates 1,570 pounds of solid waste. Fifty-five percent of this waste ends up in landfills, contributing to the second largest source of humanly-produced methane emissions in the US.***

Roughly 1/3 of solid waste comes from packaging – the colorful containers that command our attention, simplify transportation, and keep everything neat and clean.

The fluffy nests of house mice and messy abodes of sparrows demonstrate how bits of packaging can be readily reused to construct and insulate a home for protecting pinkies and hatchings. You can do the same.

- ➤ Look at labels.

- Buy products with packaging that is readily recyclable. Just because it has a recycling symbol on it doesn't mean it can be recycled in your area. For example, where I live, #6 plastic (polystyrene) is not recyclable. Check with your local waste removal service for details.

- Support recycling by purchasing recycled products such as recycled paper insulation, plastic milk carton-derived planks, and more.

- Consider creative ways to reuse old packaging. My mom likes to put labels over addresses and reuse large envelopes. I like to make wrapping paper out of brown paper bags, or use clean packaging waste for mixed media art projects.

*Sources: *Duke University Center for Sustainability and Commerce*
*   ** US EPA, 2011*

Share your creative ideas for reducing waste.

____

____

____

____

____

Purposeful repurposing

After planting the seeds for our family's organic vegetable garden, I decided to build sturdy, reusable trellises for the growing plants. I went online and checked a website that helped local people find free materials. Focusing on scrap lumber I could re-purpose to make the trellises, I discovered a motorcycle importer 45 minutes from home with "give-away wood."

What I found was hardly scrap, as the importer was giving away long pallets that had been used for transporting motorcycles from Europe to the US. They were in perfect condition, and in looking at them, I could envision their transformation into a greenhouse/tool shed.

Over the next two weeks, my wife and I made trips with a friend's trailer to pick up about 26 pallets. These became the walls, floor, and roof of the greenhouse. Another friend had dismantled his aging fence and given us the fence rails, thinking we could cut them up to use in our woodstove. The rails were long and slightly warped, but they made a fine floor.

In exchange for tearing down the lean-to beside a different friend's barn, I was offered some old corrugated metal which became both the roof of the greenhouse, as well as its north and west walls. All I had to do was caulk the nail holes to create a leak-proof roof. A length of hand-me-down heavy-mil plastic was re-purposed into the east and south walls, allowing sunlight to bathe the growing seedlings.

After the greenhouse was framed, I dismantled the remaining pallets (removing more screws and staples than I'd thought possible) and put them with reclaimed fencing wire to build trellises and stakes.

The results of this project not only make tending our garden much more convenient, but they also serve as examples of ethically re-purposing materials which still have plenty of life left in them. In our own small way, we are impacting our world in a positive way, taking a tiny bit of stress off of the world's food production and waste disposal systems. There are endless possibilities when re-purposing building materials.

— Jonathan Wright, Owner, Crocker & Springer, Ltd.

"Paper or plastic?"

*Did you know… Plastic bags can take thousands of years to decompose, but actually take up less space in landfills than paper bags?**

"Paper or plastic?" the cashier asks. Paper bags come from a renewable resource – trees raised just to be cut and processed into paper, whereas plastic bags are derived from nonrenewable petroleum.

It takes about 3 tons of wood chips to make 1 ton of pulp (using 400 parts water to 1 part pulp) along with an assortment of chemicals to produce paper. While paper may seem like a better choice, it requires a lot of resources.

The cashier waits patiently for my answer, as I fumble for a canvas bag filled with more reusable bags. "You can use the bags I brought." I smile, hoping he and his bagger share my desire to create less waste. For my grocery shopping, reusable bags replace at least 4 grocery bags per week, which saves over 200 bags per year.

- ➢ Use reusable bags and containers.

- Bring reusable canvas or expandable string bags to the store to transport purchases.

- Bring reusable containers for leftovers to your favorite restaurant.

- Purchase goods made from recycled materials whenever possible.

**Source: http://www.greenfeet.net/newsletter/debate.shtml*

List ways to reuse the bags and boxes you acquire. For example, plain paper bags make great weed blankets in the garden while strong cardboard boxes can be used for moving or storage. Be creative!

____

____

____

____

____

____

Water bottles

*Did you know... Over 60 million plastic bottles end up in landfills and incinerators every day?**

While it used to be the fad to drink a pop, many Americans are selecting a far-from-bubbly, unsweetened natural alternative, water. Consuming 70 million bottles of water each day, Americans lead the world in bottled water consumption. I know I drink it now and then – usually at social gatherings when I don't bring my reusable water bottle.

It was at one of these gatherings that a friend who happened to be sipping a bottled water told me that she purchased bottled water because she liked the taste better than water from her reusable water bottle. While I contemplated how drinking from one plastic bottle over another could be better or worse, I had to agree. I had some water bottles that made the water inside smell and taste like plastic; so I recycled them and continued to use different bottles until I found one I liked.

- ➤ Find a reusable water bottle that meets your needs.

- • Look for a bottle that is durable and practical. Soft plastics (such as HDPE #2, LDPE #4, and polypropylene #5) tend to absorb flavors from other beverages. Try aluminum. Consider a water bottle that fits in the cup holder of a car and doesn't leak in a backpack.

- • Take your water bottle along as you run errands, attend meetings, etc.

- • It may take a few minutes to put ice and water in it, but you're saving money and reducing the probability that another water bottle will end up in a landfill.

- • If you drink bottled water at a party, ask for directions to the nearest recycling bin.

**Source: Container Recycling Institute*

Since most bottled water lids are not recyclable, find ways to reuse lids for decorative or practical purposes, such as refrigerator magnets, ornaments, toys, art, and more! Sketch a few ideas here.

Seasonal Ponderings for Winter

Celebrate the unique qualities of each season. Begin in the season that corresponds with the season you pick up this book, and come back to write, draw, and reflect anytime you like. Season's greetings!

New Year's resolutions

This year, I resolved to do something I've never put into words. I decided that I would spend time outdoors every day – no matter what. As part of a "Leave No Child Inside" group, I advocate that children spend time outside every day, but don't always "take 5" to do it myself. It's not that I don't want to go outdoors, it's just that I have other responsibilities that require my attention (and plenty of excuses on cold, rainy days).

Yet, every time I look at a sunset, listen to the sweeping current of a rushing brook, or watch snow sparkle, I feel better, reminded that something larger is afoot in my life – something that makes the world beautiful every day without my help.

> Be conscious of your natural surroundings each day (not just the weather), but the birds, flowers, snowflakes, and more.

- Drink in natural light. If you don't have windows where you work, get to a window (whenever you can) to look outdoors and a door where you can go out for a while.

- Absorb bits and pieces of the natural world through as many senses as you can.

Draw what you see, feel, or experience.

Behold a perfect snowflake on the sleeve of your coat

Capture the symmetry of this snowflake, a pinecone, or the opposite branches of a tree or shrub in winter.

This is for the birds!

*Did you know... More than 40% of Americans feed backyard birds?**

Each winter, we put out a variety of foods for the birds – suet, sunflower seeds, thistle seeds, seed mix, and nuts. Fearless squirrels stuff themselves with sunflower seeds and nuts before they are shooed away.

Dark-eyed juncos and mourning doves retrieve tiny round millet seeds scattered on the ground by hasty blue jays, as sparrows huddle in the feed trough pecking open sunflower seeds one frosty winter morning. Picky cardinals simply wait for the feeder to be filled again.

Feeding songbirds helps them to survive the rigors of winter with less stress and better nutrition. If you feed songbirds in the winter, don't stop until natural food sources become readily available.

- ➢ Feed the songbirds in your neighborhood this winter.

- Clean and disinfect bird feeders once a month or more often, if needed. Use 1 part bleach to 9 parts warm water, thoroughly scrub and air dry.

- Purchase seed in small quantities and keep it in a cool, dry place as seed can attract rodents or harbor bugs.

- Participate in a bird count organized by the Audubon Society, Cornell Lab of Ornithology, or local nature centers to learn more about birds.

**Source: National Audubon Society*

Keep track of the number of birds you see the same day each winter and do the same for other seasons. Write and draw what you see.

____

____

____

____

A day at the zoo

*Did you know... The lowest temperature on record for Chicago was -24°F in 1985?**

Though summer is a popular time to visit the zoo, I like to visit in winter, too. Much like the African and Asian animals confined to balmy indoor exhibits, I sometimes feel limited by this "most wonderful time of the year" – limited by diminishing daylight, freezing temperatures, and somewhat uncooperative weather conditions.

I cannot change the weather, but I can work to change the way I see winter. Living outside of Chicago for over 20 years, I learned to celebrate the beauty of delicate ice crystals and blankets of snow.

> ➤ Discover something to appreciate about winter.

- Remove the limitations attached to the seasons and work to see their necessity to the environment, your local economy, and the world. If your surroundings were any different than they are, the effect might be catastrophic to humanity. For example, imagine what it would be like for Chicago, IL to have the weather of Tampa, FL.

- Share the joy of the season with others through writing, a phone call, or other meaningful communication.

**Source: The Weather Channel (www.weather.com)*

Write a haiku – a nature-oriented Japanese style of unrhymed poetry with 5 syllables in line 1, 7 syllables in line 2, and 5 syllables in line 3.

____

____

____

____

____

____

Artificial or real?

Did you know... One acre of evergreen trees produce enough oxygen for 18 people? Evergreens also grow in soils that typically don't support other crops.

Why do we cut down trees every year for a week or two of indoor holiday decor? Is it a tradition, something fun, or a little bit of both?

I grew up with an artificial tree purchased at an after-Christmas sale when I was very young. Every year, we'd take it out of storage, put it together, decorate it, enjoy it, and then put it away. The nonrenewable petroleum-based tree was a steadfast part of our family's decor until my mom gave it away over 30 years later. If a teacher had not accepted it for her classroom, I fear the old tree would have ended up in a landfill. Real trees don't have this problem.

Recyclable and biodegradable, real trees can be used for wildlife habitat or converted into wood chips.

➤ Plan ahead.

- If you are going to buy a live evergreen for your yard, make sure you have the right soil conditions. If not, consider getting a tree in a container which can be given to a friend.

- If purchasing a cut tree, make sure your waste service will pick up and recycle it, or contact your local parks department to see where you can drop it off. <u>Never</u> dump Christmas trees at parks or other public places.

Take a moment to record the qualities you want in a tree. Are you looking for an interesting color? Blue spruce has a unique bluish green color. Would you like soft needles? White pine has long, soft needles.

____

____

____

____

____

____

Deck the halls

Did you know... Americans throw away 25% more trash between Thanksgiving and New Year's than any other time of year?

My cousin loves Christmas and has three Christmas trees she keeps decorated each year. Two have ornaments she has collected through the years and the third is a smaller tree with decorations she makes using junk. It is fun to see what she creates.

- ➤ See what you can make from "junk."

- Take a look at the stuff you throw out. Can you fashion something new from something you might normally throw away?

- Borrow a recycled or nature craft book from the library or check the internet for ideas.

- Try making a gift for a friend or an ornament for decorating the tree. Be creative, mix media and have fun!

**Source: www.use-less-stuff.com/ULSDAY/42ways*

Sketch ideas for items you'd like to reuse.

I started decorating trees with plastic that could not be recycled. Making a garland with multi-colored plastic bottle lids, I began to look at various other things that could be reused. I found plastic bear-shaped honey containers could be filled with soil or sand to make them look like little brown bears.

The first tree I decorated was an artificial tree that I took down to our village's public works department. They loved it! A cousin who saw my work asked me to make one for his nature center, and our garden club made one for a camp that serves children with disabilities. Now there are groups of children that continue this tradition in our area.

— Lee Cain, Garden Editor (retired), The Cincinnati Post

Holidays

*Did you know... In 2015, the average American shopper was expected to spend $805 on holiday shopping?**

Holidays, or Holy Days evoke memories of all kinds – music, conversation, good food, and laughter – lots of laughter. When I think of my family, I have pretty positive memories of the holidays until I grew up, got married, and became part of another person's family. Everyone was nice, but I didn't really know what they liked or wanted.

Partly because I am unforgivably frugal and partly because I didn't know what material thing constituted the "perfect" gift, I dreaded the idea of giving the wrong gift, so one holiday, I took a risk and made raspberry preserves.

I had never made the stuff and really didn't know how long to cook it so it wouldn't either remain sauce or become a ball of seeds and goo. As I gave it to everyone, I hoped they would like it, but wondered if it was really a "good" gift.

The conversation began to swirl around the small jars like steam from the canning bath. Raspberry preserves were not just food for my family of in-laws, but a reminder of Grandma Anderson, a special person (and extraordinary cook) everyone loved. How many gifts have you ever had do that?

➢ Listen to your heart.

• Keep it simple.

• Look at giving as an opportunity to share something that will meet another's need. What may be good for one person, may not be good for another.

• Make a donation to a charity in the name of a loved one.

• Make something yourself. A card with a beautiful picture and a special poem you wrote shows you have taken time to reflect on the special qualities of another.

Source: National Retail Federation

Give without expecting something in return

What are some gifts you receive from the natural world? Think BIG and small. Example: Plants give us oxygen.

____

____

____

____

____

____

____

What are some ways you can help the natural world using my gifts or talents? Example: I can use writing and art to connect others with the wonders of nature.

____

____

____

____

____

____

Beyond the hamster wheel

Did you know… Gymnasium use dates back to the ancient Greeks training for athletic contests such as the Olympics?

Indoor exercise continues to be the fashion, as health clubs and fitness centers pop up like so many mushrooms in the fertile soil of bodily discontent.

Whenever I visit a store with animals – be it a pet store, a feed store, or one of those large box stores that sells everything – I marvel at what it must be like to live in a container. Walking by a fitness center, I looked through a window and saw a man climbing stairs on a step machine, a woman pacing vigorously on a treadmill, and various other people exercising within a glass box for humans. I thought back to a hamster I saw exercising on a wheel in its cage. Was there a difference? I couldn't see one. As people fought for the closest parking space to the center, and then hopped on an elevator to get to the fitness area, I wondered why they were not outdoors doing what I was doing – running errands (on foot), ice skating at the park, sledding or skiing with their kids – going beyond the walls of a temperature-regulated atmosphere into the bright chill of a northern day. This is not to say that fitness centers are not good places to work out when severe temperatures or icy conditions preclude safe outdoor pursuits. In fact, I like such places. My concern lies in the appearance that there are so many people that never seem to exercise beyond the walls of a building.

> Exercise outdoors.

- Take friends outdoors to enjoy hiking, skiing, and other seasonal sports.

- Have fun exploring different ecosystems in your area, while staying on designated trails to preserve the natural beauty all around.

How does going outdoors change your exercise experience?

____

____

____

____

____

____

Shoveling

Every year, I'm grateful that I can shovel snow. This may sound odd, especially in an age of plows and blowers, but there remains something very special about shoveling a sidewalk or driveway yourself. Perhaps it's the chill of winter air on your cheeks, confirming that you're still alive – the bright sunshine beaming off the stark whiteness of glistening snow, or the cloudless blue skies of winter.

Where I grew up in southern Ohio, we didn't have much snow, but every time we did, it was gorgeous (until I started driving). Due to a combination of icy conditions and limited resources, roads were frequently left unplowed for the sun to melt. Eventually moving to southern Michigan, central Minnesota, and northern Illinois, I observed a different mentality toward snow. Due to extended periods of cold temperatures, something had to be done, so a battalion of plow trucks would treat major corridors at the sign of the first snowflake. There were no excuses for businesses not to be open or children not to be in school during snowy weather that would cripple other parts of the country. This was winter, and winter was part of life.

Shoveling is a visceral ritual that puts you ankle-deep in the elements, while swirling winds nip at exposed flesh. It's just you and a tool – a tool that scrapes the ground, making little if any other sound – daring Mother Nature to keep you indoors.

> ➢ Take in the beauty of this enchanted landscape.

- If it does not snow where you live, you can participate in this activity by beholding the subtle changes of season in your own backyard.

- If you are not physically able to shovel, enjoy the view.

Express your feelings about winter through painting, drawing, photography or writing, just as others have done for generations. Use the space below.

Tadpoles in February

Did you know… It can take up to 3 years for a bullfrog to mature from egg to adult?

It was the end of February and the ground was covered with patchy spots of snow and ice. My children rushed inside to tell me they had seen tadpoles wiggling in the bottom of the pond. I just shook my head not believing that tadpoles would be active in a pond containing ice.

"Come see," they beckoned. Trudging through the ice-crusted snow at the edge of the pond, I was stunned by the sight of a mass of large, wildly wiggling tadpoles. I edged closer and lost track of where I was walking. My boot pierced the ice and quickly disappeared into dark muck, as I lunged forward. The children laughed as I removed the wet boot covered with black mud and stringy plants from the place it had become unnaturally planted. I continued to marvel.

➤ Embrace unexpected wonders.

• Explore the outdoors like someone who has never been outside.

• Share your nature discoveries with others.

Write or draw about an unexpected wonder today.

____

____

____

____

____

Birding

Birding is activity you can enjoy for a lifetime. Even young children can watch birds. My mom found out my brother needed glasses when he said he couldn't see the birds outside the breakfast room window. Thankfully, he could hear them.

Bird songs and calls resonate with individuals who cannot see, providing intriguing landscapes for perceiving the natural world. Can you think of your favorite bird song? Does it sound like a flute or a hearty laugh? Listen.

- Let the beauty and grace of birds inspire you to rise above the obstacles that seem to mar your path.

- Borrow or purchase a good quality, lightweight pair binoculars and a field guide to identify the birds you see.

- Look for birds in your backyard or visit a nearby natural area.

- Attend a program at twilight, dawn, or after dark at nearby nature centers, park districts, or Audubon clubs to see different birds with people who know and love birds.

- Plant native flowers and trees (especially adapted to the soil, water and light conditions in your yard), which will provide habitat for birds.

Keep track of the birds you see each season.

Seasonal Ponderings for Springtime

Skunk cabbage

*Did you know… Skunk cabbage can produce its own heat. It can maintain a core temperature 59-86 degrees F higher than surrounding frigid northern temperatures.**

Early each spring, skunk cabbage appears in local fens. Looking like miniature Little Red Riding Hoods, the mysterious dark red flower emerges in running water and wet edges of slightly alkaline wetlands. A harbinger of spring, the red hood-like spathe of this flower can be seen amid late snows asserting the end of winter and reassuring other wildflowers that it will soon be their time to bloom.

The stream is green with leafy watercress while the ground remains barren except for small pillows of moss amid once colorful fall leaves.

Spring will come, but not for a while. The air is chilly with the last desperate biting winds of winter, threatening one more snow – maybe an inch, maybe a little more. The skunk cabbage flower will weather the storm and disappear as tightly curled bright green leaves unfold into a plant that looks like cabbage (without the head), flourishing verdantly until the wilting heat of summer arrives.

- ➢ Be a harbinger of spring.

- Express the renewal of spring through your thoughts and actions.

- Appreciate the subtle colors of tree bark and not-so-subtle mosses, lichens, and colorful jelly fungi which give late winter color and beauty unique to this season.

**Source: Roger Knutson, Luther College, Department of Biology Emeritus Faculty*

Capture what you see in the space provided here.

Baby owls

Did you know... Great horned owls reside as far north as the Arctic tundra and as far south as the tropical rain forests of Central and South America.

For eight consecutive years in early March, you could see people standing on the sidewalk near the Kane County Courthouse looking through binoculars and spotting scopes at a nest containing 2–3 great horned owlets.

The fuzzy gray birds didn't seem to mind the attention, but their mother kept a watchful eye. From 2005–2013, she laid eggs in a tree near the center of town, letting birdwatchers and spectators alike enjoy a glimpse of nature commonly hidden from human eyes.

- ➤ Look up

- Acknowledge weather, air, sunlight, breezes, animals, nests, bird songs, and the earth beneath your feet.

- Consider your role as the guardian of this special place.

As you look at your surroundings, outline what you can do to improve them, to provide better living conditions for yourself, others, and the wildlife that depends on you.

____

____

____

____

____

____

____

____

Spring

Did you know… In the Northern Hemisphere, on the first day of spring (March 20 or 21 depending on the year) the hours of daylight are equivalent to the hours of darkness.

In spring, leaves of the cottonwood rustle gently in the breeze as small green bead-like seed pods prepare to release white fluffy seeds. The scenery becomes dreamy with wispy white bits of cotton-covered seeds mingling with the wind. It's spring-time in the bottomlands. Orioles and warblers are migrating through the area as great blue herons and belted kingfishers settle in.

Spring is a time for renewal and resurrection, as green shoots appear above snow-pressed autumn leaves and once chilling winds of winter give place to shower-sprinkled breezes. Spring calls us out of our cozy burrows to plant flowers, work on the garden, and spend more time outdoors in increasingly longer sunlit days.

> ➢ Be transformed, like the flowers.

- Pursue enriching activities that will help you grow as a person and bloom as a flower in the garden of humanity.

- Look at the wildflowers in your community each week and consider how much they change in a short period of time without negative consequences.

Share transformations you've observed in yourself or your surroundings.

____

____

____

____

____

____

____

Mother Goose & Father, too!

Did you know... Canada geese adopt goslings?

One spring I received a call from a worker in an office building near the nature center where I worked. Apparently, a goose had laid eggs on a balcony overlooking the pond and the flightless goslings had no way to safely join their parents several stories down.

Shepherding the fuzzy young birds into a large cardboard box, I took them to the pond, hoping that they would either find their parents or be adopted by other geese. Without the care and protection of an adult goose, they could be easily become dinner for snapping turtles, predatory fish, fox, coyote, or even neighborhood dogs.

Within minutes, a couple of adult geese on the other side of the pond spotted the goslings. Gracefully, the adults crossed the pond to the meet young birds and then together, they swam to another part of the pond. All of the goslings were accepted.

Were these adults the goslings' biological parents or had they been adopted? I would never know, but I was certain the goslings would receive the care they needed to grow and flourish.

> ➢ Care for those in need.

- Adopt a family or individual in need through the local crisis center, school district, or senior citizen center.

- Donate holiday gifts to Toys For Tots. Visit www.toysfortots.org

- Send a gift to a soldier. Visit www.uso.org

**Source: NationalGeographic.com*

List some talents or strengths you have not yet shared with your community, and ways you can benefit others with these qualities.

____

____

____

____

____

A bit of soil

Pitchfork in hand, I head outside to face the vegetable garden – a large rectangle that spends the winter alternately freezing and thawing. The soil looks compressed and lifeless, except for a few green weeds. I plunge the old wooden-handled pitch-fork into unyielding darkness to remove weeds and loosen the soil where I plan to plant. Once the person who would use a pitchfork to break up the soil in an entire garden, I now use it sparingly.

Knowing that the more I chop up soil, the more I destroy the soil's natural structure and promote weedy growth, I have been trying to change my ways. Worms wiggle through tunnels, now exposed to the light, rushing to escape a waiting robin. A few become the plump bird's next meal, stretching to stay in the ground, but unsuccessfully succumbing. Native bees with stingers too tiny to harm me, fly from tiny holes in the soil that has not been turned. This soil does not look like the dreamy loam shown in gardens on TV, but is teeming with life.

- ➢ Preserve what is good, and improve what you can.

- If parts of your life feel static and unwieldy, take a mental pitchfork (a real one would hurt!) and get to the heart of what needs to be addressed.

- Break up the large clods (challenges) into smaller more workable bits and make a commitment to reach your goals every day.

List the challenges you'd like to address this week.

____

____

____

____

____

____

____

Through the eyes of an oak

Did you know... The boundary oak tree once found at Lincoln's birthplace lived for approximately 195 years?

When I was a child, I'd seen a massive white oak tree standing reverently near a small brook between a home believed to have been Abraham Lincoln's birthplace and a sunken spring. Upon returning to Hodgenville, Kentucky over 30 years later (on Lincoln's 200th birthday), a cross-section of this great tree was on display. It died in 1976, and was finally removed in 1986.

The young oak had seen the world change as indigenous people and early settlers traversed its landscape, a forest became a farm, and a farm became a park. It had seen the early years of a small child who would leave his mark in history, war, and peace. A silent sentinel, the boundary oak was firmly rooted in the past, but connected to the present, providing food and shelter for wildlife, along with a unique historical perspective to human visitors.

- ➢ Visit an old tree or place in your community and consider its historical roots.

- Imagine what it has seen.

- Record what you experience and how it makes you feel.

Source: National Park Service

Create a list of your happiest memories along with ways you've grown as a person. Trees are not the only ones to grow.

____

____

____

____

____

____

____

Under a log

A tree's life is not over when it falls down and becomes a log on the forest floor.
— Anne Hunter, author of What's Under a Log

While logs do not really look exciting from the surface, they are treasure troves of life. One day as I was walking through the woods, I rolled over a log. Formerly part of a nearby cherry tree, it was as big around as my thigh, but denser and heavier.

I'm not sure how long it had been lying there, but telltale bits of wood indicated it was being inhabited and consumed by something. I turned the heavy log slowly and carefully to discover its secrets. A centipede darted into the soil, a toddling black ground beetle scurried for cover, and the tip of an earthworm (not sure which end!) stuck above the soil. Under other logs I had seen slugs, slug eggs, and millipedes, but not this one – not today. I carefully rolled the log back into its original resting place and headed for home.

> ➤ Look for the hidden treasures in your life.

- Consider what you're hiding under a log – talents, beauty, and grandeur. Find ways to share these wonderful gifts with others.

- If there are hurts from the past that need to be healed, deal with them. Get help. Let sadness and painful memories disappear like a decomposing log.

Write about your treasures and triumphs.

____

____

____

____

____

____

____

____

A garden for Daisy

Whether expected or unexpected, loss is a roller coaster of emotions that is a deeply personal process with many, many variables. Feel God's omnipresence by letting Him in, and finding comfort in community. – Rabbi Chase Foster

To really appreciate Daisy, you had to know the smiling 5-year-old girl with sunny blonde hair and dancing blue eyes. I watched her grow up through holiday letters from her parents the first five years of her life. Knowing her parents had buried her stillborn sister a few years earlier, I saw her as a ray of hope who would live a long and healthy life with two of the best parents anyone could have. This made her passing even more of a shock. Her mom and I cried over long distance lines together unable to console each other. Daisy was her daughter, and I felt my friend's devastation as much as a friend can. I had to do something special for Daisy, but what?

With spring quickly approaching, I decided to plant flowers. No one in my neighborhood knew about Daisy, but I planted flowers in the neighborhood for her. I planted flowers at the school for her. Every time I planted flowers that year, I thought of her and how the native perennial flowers would return in beauty for years to come.

> ➤ Find comfort in sharing the beauty and generosity of someone who passed away through the good things you grow.

- Plant native wildflowers to beautify your community.

- Grow vegetables to feed others. Consider raising heirlooms so you can reuse seed year after year.

Draw or write about your feelings.

____

____

____

____

Growing beyond grief

Laura has been my friend since high school. Long before Bill was her husband or even a boyfriend, I accompanied him for his sophomore trombone recital. I didn't want to. A big bear of a man, Bill was nice, but not my type.

After he and Laura got married, I began to appreciate Bill's uniqueness. As a professional symphony trombonist, he gave music lessons. As the father of two sons, he was extremely active in Boy Scouts.

In May of the year when their eldest son was graduating from high school, Bill was killed in a car accident. Grieved and shocked, I went to my garden to work and find comfort. With my hands in the dirt, I decided to remember Bill by planting a row of sunflowers – different colors and kinds – but all tall and sturdy like he had been.

When I went to his funeral and spoke with my friend, Laura, I told her about the sunflowers. Although surrounded by many of Bill's friends and admirers, she took time to listen and enjoy the thought of Bill's sunflower memorial.

I continued to watch the flowers grow that summer, remembering Bill. Like him, the sunflowers were big and practical. After the flowers were done blooming and their petals began to shrivel, some of the seeds fed animals while some fell to the earth to germinate the following spring. In the language of flowers, sunflowers symbolize strength with their thick stems and positivity as their large blossoms turn to follow the sun.

Bill's seeds of kindness and instruction, which he so generously sowed in the hearts of his family, students, and community, have continued his legacy.

— Laura Knoerr, Professional Writer/Playwright

Food for thought

*Did you know… Approximately 26% of Earth's ice-free land is used for livestock grazing and 33 percent of croplands are used for livestock feed production.**

With tight economic times come shortages aplenty. After the holidays, food bank supplies dwindle, as credit card bills soar. Countless people complain of added girth, while others wonder where they will get their next meal – hunger and obesity are pervasive.

A few years ago, a woman started a community garden at a church on the outskirts of town. She and her volunteers from church and town are now donating the food they grow to a local food pantry. Another woman is starting a community garden in a park near her home and a team from the library is following suit, asking food pantry staff what they need and providing fresh food for those who need it most.

> ➤ Work right where you are to provide food for local food pantries, soup kitchens, and charities.

- People need to eat other days beside Thanksgiving. Host a food drive during the "off-season" of March or April.

- If you're trying to cut unhealthy foods out of your diet, put the money you would have spent on something unhealthy in a jar to donate for feeding those who are hungry.

- Volunteer to gather or distribute food, or work on a community garden to provide vegetables and herbs to feed people suffering with hunger where you live.

**Source: Food and Agriculture Organization of the United Nations, Sustainability Pathways*

It is natural for everyone to have enough food to eat. Write about how your actions to feed others have enriched you.

____

____

____

____

The perfect garden

Did you know… Potager (pronounced /po-tah-zhayr/) gardening has its roots in medieval history and refers to colorful French kitchen gardens combining flowers, herbs, fruits and vegetables in the same space?

Potager gardening requires a different mindset than traditional vegetable gardening because careful crop rotations are instrumental in keeping the potager garden looking good throughout the year. Informal, sensory-driven counterparts to the formal gardens surrounding great châteaux, potagers are islands of diverse vegetation providing essential wildlife habitat along with ample quantities of fruits and vegetables for a gardener to enjoy with family and friends.

- ➤ Get ready to grow!

- Look at your garden space. What can you grow successfully in this space given soil, climate, and other challenges? Explore companion planting or placing plants together that will complement each other's growth while staving off pests.

- Consider plants that will add color and interest from early spring through fall. Include self-seeding native plants and genetically-diverse heirloom varieties for interesting, tasty alternatives. You'll have to thin plants later, but then your friends and neighbors can get into gardening, too!

- Confine aggressive plants to containers or areas bordered by lawn or rock. Add other items of interest to your garden, such as homemade stepping stones, and a tepee or trellis to hold vines.

- Recruit your children, nieces, nephews or grandchildren to help. Gardening puts children in touch with nature and gives them healthy snacks, too! Each year, each member of our family lists what he or she would like to have in the garden and we plant accordingly.

- Tend your garden 15-20 minutes every morning, removing weeds, providing water or planting seeds.

Brainstorm ideas

Create a layout for what you'd like to grow in your garden:

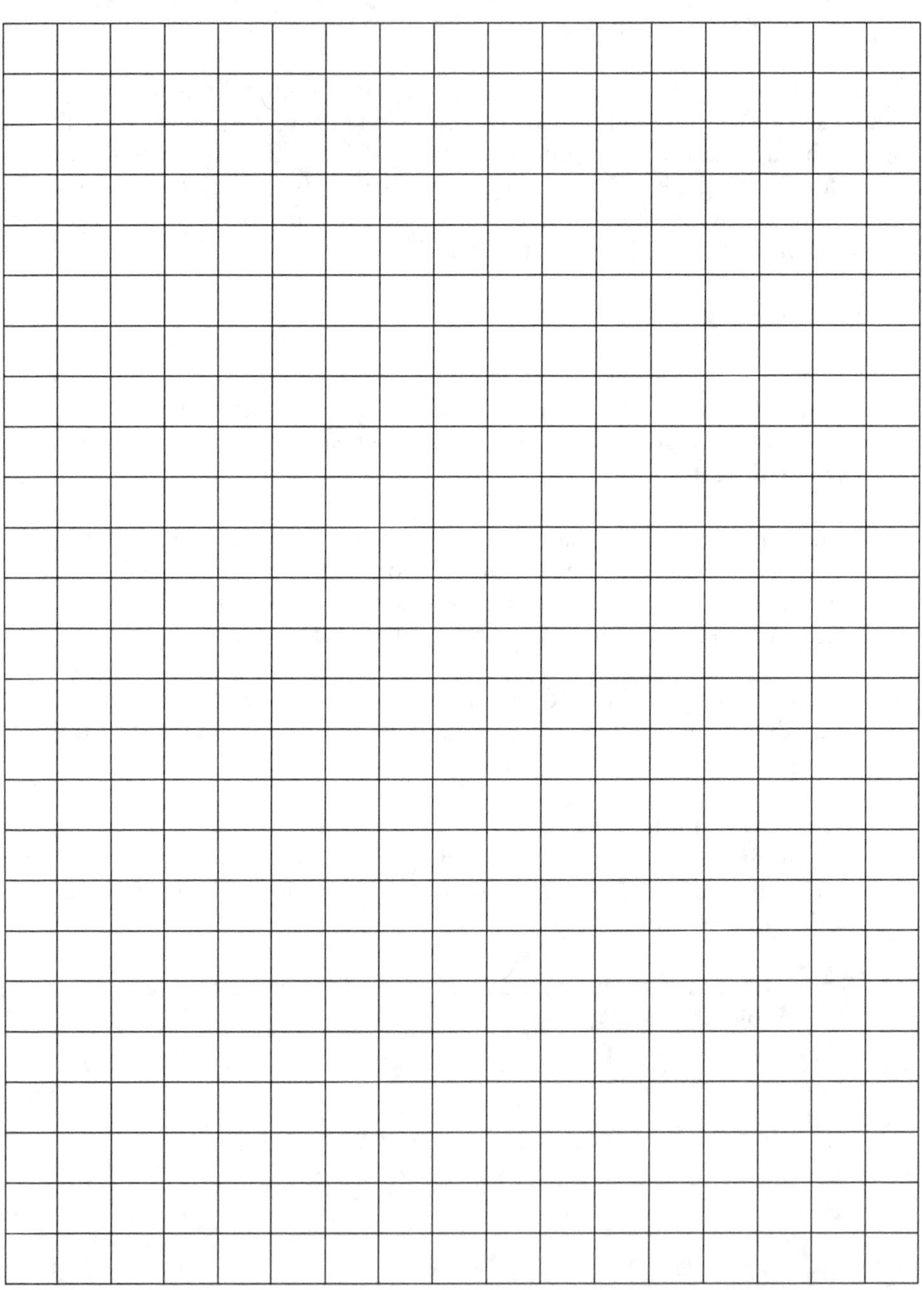

Essential connections

I love to go camping. It brings me closer to nature and the heart of humanity. The sun wakes me up with its quiet appearance, and puts me to sleep with its equally picturesque disappearance. I get to cross paths with strangers first thing in the morning, unwashed, uncombed, and still wearing the fragrance of the previous night's campfire. Gentle smiles cover their sleepy faces.

I may see these people again or only once in a lifetime. I know nothing of them nor do they know of me. We are equals in spite of the cars we drive, the homes we inhabit, or the lives we lead. Camping is more than tents and sleeping bags, it's bats flying in the dusky sky, a great horned owl calling in the darkness, moths flitting around outdoor lights, and a chorus of birds welcoming a new day. It saturates the senses with constant color, sound, beauty, and wonder reminding of us that we are small parts of a something bigger.

- ➤ Go camping!

- Meet your neighbors and the park staff where you are camping. Explore and enjoy lesser known parts of the park with the help of park naturalists. If you meet people at the campground with common interests, encourage them to join you.

- Capture your experience outdoors through creative expression. One of the most beautiful examples of this occurred when I was camping in the Black Hills of South Dakota and heard someone singing. His strong voice filled the valley with a richness that complemented the rocky scenery.

Draw something you saw or felt, or maybe even write a song!

Seasonal Ponderings for Summertime

Rise with the sun and rest beneath the stars

Reflect on how these experiences make you feel using words and/or art.

Appearances

A few years ago, some friends gave me a dill plant containing black swallowtail cat-erpillars. Having never raised butterflies, I was thrilled at the prospect of watching these colorful caterpillars turn into beautiful butterflies, but wondered how long I'd have to wait. One day I looked in the bug container, only to find two dead-looking caterpillars clinging to the roof, their bodies in lifeless "J" formations.

What had I done wrong? I resolved to find out, leaving the caterpillars where they were to do some research.

By the time I returned, the dead-looking caterpillars were gone – replaced by beautiful chrysalids. Would everything be okay now? I wondered with doubt. Watching the chrysalids change from green to black, I feared the worst, thinking it might be best to remove the chrysalids the next day.

As I peered in the container the following morning, I could see what appeared to be a small, but brilliant black butterfly hanging from a chrysalis and another small butterfly clutching the lid of the bug box. In spite of their questionable appearances, both butterflies had survived their life journey and were ready to be released, so I wished them well and let them go.

- ➤ Question assumptions based on appearances.

- A caterpillar about to enter its chrysalis looks dead. The senses would tell us that the situation is hopeless.

- Shed the chrysalis of limitation. Do the good things that are natural for you to do and soar.

Write about your experiences beyond the chrysalis today.

Clouds

Everywhere I've ever lived I've looked to the sky – from fog-blanketed mountains to dawning light on farm fields and sunsets into the depths of still waters. Clouds complete the picture, giving the sky a temporary ceiling and breaking up the blueness of the heavens — dancing and billowing, boiling angry with storms, and disappearing.

In 1803 Luke Howard, an early weather watcher, used Latin words to describe different types of clouds.

Cirrus – wispy, feathery, mare's tail-like clouds

Nimbus – rain clouds

Cumulus – piled clouds

Stratus – layered clouds

Today the sky is the color of an eastern bluebird, brilliant and crisp. As the day progresses, wispy cirrus clouds appear frozen in time. The sky changes, but its beauty is undiminished.

- ➤ Look at the clouds like a child.

- Marvel at the shapes and colors of clouds.

- Learn to identify the clouds in your area.

Draw your favorite cloud formations below.

Squishing bugs

I can't say I squished a lot of bugs when I was a kid, but I can remember getting pretty upset when a wasp would get in and buzz around the house. Was it the wasp's ominous sound or just the knowledge that it could sting multiple times? It's hard to say, but I did not appreciate that bug. Years later, I did not choose a career exterminating wasps, but educating people about nature and encouraging them not to squish bugs.

Little did I know that my job as a naturalist would make a beeline back to the fray of buzzing creatures – this time the buzz was from honeybees. The opportunity to get up close and personal with honeybees came when I worked at a nature center. An experienced beekeeper asked if I'd like to help him install an observation hive.

As I put on a white coverall, a fabric screen veil, a pith helmet, and long, thick leather gloves, I began to anticipate the encounter with a sense of giddy excitement. The white outfit wasn't going to keep me safe. The bees would still buzz and their stingers would still be able to sting. As we approached the box, the beekeeper began to pour smoke on the tense little bugs. The bees continued to buzz, but didn't seem as bothered by our presence.

The beekeeper removed a frame from the box and asked me to look for the queen. I searched amid lines of wiggling bodies, but I couldn't find her. The beekeeper took back the frame and looked himself. A queen must be present to provide leadership and lay eggs for generations of bees to come. The beekeeper eventually found the large female and finished installing the hive. I appreciated the opportunity to get closer to bees without getting stung.

> ➢ Get beyond the buzz of every day life to eliminate fear.

- Fear can have no part in your relationships with others. While I am still careful with bees and wasps, I no longer fear them like I did when I was a child. The other day, I let a bee go that was riding on a plant in my car.

- Be grateful for the work of bees and wasps – pollinating food crops, flowers, and trees that beautify the earth.

Share something you've observed about an insect.

____

____

____

____

Worried flowers

The pale purple coneflowers are blooming where I work, while the purple coneflowers at home are just beginning to stretch out their petals. Their unfoldment seems effortless and steady to the casual bystander. Each day, the petals unfurl a bit more of their rich beauty. They show no concern for shelter, nourishment, or water. They simply grow.

Yet, I worry sometimes.

Am I not as cared for and as loved as the flower I behold in the garden? The flower shows no sign of worry, why should I? Like the flower, I am here for a reason – a unique purpose. You are, too. Worry distracts us from this purpose.

- ➤ Flourish like the flower, and refuse to entertain worry.

- Work hard, help others, and expect good. Replace all vestiges of worry with gratitude.

- Explore the role of faith in your life – spend quiet time in nature, attend a religious service, and listen.

Write about what you can do, and then do it!

Chicory

Did you know… Individual chicory flowers only bloom for one day?

Chicory, a spindly green plant with purplish blue flowers, grows along roadsides throughout much of the US. Nicknamed ragged sailors, chicory flowers look handsome at the beginning of the day and tattered by the end as each individual flower takes turns blooming from mid-summer through early fall. Their transient beauty reminds the beholder to live in the present.

Too often distracted by thoughts of the past or wishes for the future, we miss the special nature of today and the moments that make today special.

> ➤ Be present for the present.

- Be grateful for every moment of beauty, spirit, and light.

- Share this beauty and wonder with others as you feel inspired.

Try drawing a picture or writing a poem.

Lightning bugs

Every July, lightning bugs come out in the backyard, flashing signals to their mates and capturing the wonder of all. How amazing it is to see a little insect (that has the ability to produce a discernible light in the darkness) transport everyone in its presence back to a state of youthful wonder!

Lightning bugs don't start glowing as adults, but begin sharing their light as larvae called glowworms. While I had always heard about glowworms, I'd never seen them until this past summer. Hidden in the dark grasses of a balmy summer night, the well-named larvae shone like threads of starlight on earth.

How often are we turning on our "lights" – shining lovely qualities for all to see? Are such lights sometimes only reserved for certain others like the lightning bug communicating with its mate?

- ➤ Shine right where you are!

- Express something that makes you happy and will bring joy to others – smiling, sharing a good thought, etc.

- You do not have to be a certain age to shine; the lightning bug shines as a larvae. Teach children to shine in their lives through everything they do.

Write about shining moments in your day.

____

____

____

____

____

____

____

____

Worms

Did you know... There are no terrestrial earthworms native to Minnesota? At least 15 species have been introduced so far.

Worms aerate, mix, and enrich soil while removing the spongy organic "duff" layer that provides habitat for wildlife along with an essential growing medium for native wildflowers.

Seemingly insignificant, worms are eating machines that alter ecosystems where they have been introduced. Initially coming to the US in the soil of plants brought by settlers in the late 1800's, worms continue to invade areas where people dump bait, install plants, bring in dirt, or drive off-road vehicles.

- Look for the duff layer in your local natural areas.

- Learn about invasive worms where you live.

- Try hot composting, which is done with microorganisms (instead of worms), to provide soil for gardening and indoor plantings.

- Give worm bait to fish or other worm-loving pets instead of dumping it in the soil.

- Wash dirt-covered tires and boots between adventures.

Source: Minnesota Department of Natural Resources

Use this space to keep notes about composting.

____

____

____

____

____

____

____

Seasonal Ponderings for Autumn

A walk in the woods

*Did you know... As early as 285 B.C. Theophrastus, a Greek philosopher and natural scientist, described the shedding of leaves we call fall**

It's October and the leaves are changing colors – burnt red, smiley face yellow, and chocolate hues of fragile crispness. Blanketing the ground in preparation for winter, the patchwork of leaves cover the tiny seeds of woodland knotweed and thumb-nail-sized acorns.

As I walk through the woods, I see holes left by squirrels among rain-matted leaves, exposing small circles of rich, black earth. A tapestry of color is warmed by the sun and chilled by the descent of darkness. The autumn woods is an awe-inspiring place with periodic bits of color swirling against a stark blue sky.

> ➤ Observe the season.

- Rejoice in the beauty of the season.

- Escape controlled indoor climes to feel chill, heat, breeze, or drizzle.

Write about what makes this day and season special to you.

Autumn is beautiful

Create a collage of autumn leaf rubbings or prints.
　To make a leaf rubbing, place a leaf (textured or vein-side up) beneath this page and rub with a flat crayon. To make a leaf print, gently color the textured vein-side of a leaf with a marker then place it on the page, cover with another piece of paper, and press.

Gulls in the parking lot

Did you know… Many of the birds we dub "seagulls" never live near nor visit the ocean.

About 20 herring gulls paraded around the vacant parking lot in front of a former grocery store. It was a cool October day following a rainy weekend and the gulls were stopping for a while to consider whether they should stay for the winter or migrate a little further south.

Perhaps they would be ambitious and fly to Arkansas, Mississippi, Louisiana, or eastern Mexico for the winter, but for now they seemed to be wandering on a large square of asphalt in northern Illinois, contemplating their next move.

One gull broke the rhythm with a hop while another added vocal accompaniment. The rest seemed to roam aimlessly. Occasionally, a gull would take off and land, just changing its perspective, but never leaving the group. The parade continued.

While a flock of gulls in a parking lot may appear to be aimless and uninspired, they may be resting, preparing for the next leg of a journey, and spending time with their family. Relaxation is not the opposite of work, but a way to stay sane when everything around you seems aflutter.

- Give yourself a break.

- Take a hint from the gulls, and spend time with those you love.

- If you can't take a vacation, rest right where you are.

In the field

Did you know... There are over 5 million breeding geese in the US. *

One day I parked the car in a lot just off a major road. A remnant soybean field sep-
arated me from the busy road, and construction had begun for new businesses in
the field behind us. The sun disappeared and darkness covered the landscape.

Gradually small faces with dark marble-like eyes and distinctive black cheeks
popped out of the soybean field by the road. I wondered how long they had been
there, as I considered how many times I had passed that field and never noticed any
activity.

North of this former farm, I saw geese pop up again – this time in a cornfield. I
could not help but wonder how many other things I'd missed seeing over the course
of the day.

- ➤ Experience as much of the natural world as you can.

- • Take a break and go outside for a few minutes.

- • Walk in the light, take a breath of fresh air, listen to the rustle of leaves, or
  watch a bird soar.

Source: US Fish & Wildlife Service (2013)

How do the observations you make in the natural world relate to other aspects of
your every day life?

____

____

____

____

____

____

____

____

Fall migration

Did you know… In its GO TO 2040, Chicago Metropolitan Agency for Planning (CMAP) is recommending the preservation of an additional 150,000 acres of open space in the seven county Chicago region to more parks, greenways, and access to nature?

As trees change colors and leaves drift across the fields, I get in the car and head to the country. It is a tradition that hearkens back to my family's annual autumn visits with a friend in Kentucky, eating her watermelon rind pickles and buttery biscuits, marveling over the beauty of persimmons, and picking handfuls of goldenrod – a bittersweet goodbye to summer and a celebration of fall.

Though my migratory patterns have changed, my need to see open space has not. Each year the route to the apple orchard changes from what was a fairly quiet country road to an expanded venue with new strip malls and subdivisions blighting the once productive agrarian landscape. I question the planning and forethought of these now booming counties and feel concern for their future as well as my fellow migrant birds, dependent upon the once open land for their journey.

> ➤ Be a voice in your community

- Get to know your neighbors before they decide to sell the farm. Encourage them to consider farm preservation options such as conservation easements or working lands trusts.

- Get to know the developers who come to your area. You will find many of them have good intentions, but would benefit from a better understanding of the dynamics of your community.

- Stay up-to-date on zoning and planning. Encourage local government officials to think about the long-run and the costs associated with providing expanded services to new subdivisions.

- Consider running for the county board or participating in meetings.

The future lies in the choices made today

When two of my brothers-in-law were dealing with health problems, my wife's family asked me to take over the dairy operation because I had been helping on weekends and really enjoyed the work. We milked 90 cows twice a day, while my other brother-in-law was responsible for 1,000 acres in crops (mostly corn).

Eighty acres was the size of a typical farm in Wisconsin 100 years ago. In the 1980's we were milking 90 cows twice a day; anymore it's 900 cows that you're milking. When we put in 1,000 acres of corn, now you need to put in 10,000 acres or more of corn. It's a really different world from the family farms I was a part of.

The family farm I worked for over a year was sold in the mid-1980s along with the rest of our family's farms. A "green line" that limited sprawl for 20 years was removed after the turn of the 21st century. One farm has become a golf course, one has become a landfill, and one has become a housing development.

— Dr. Noel Rudie, Senior Manager Process & Package Development, Michael Foods

Share ways to help your community retain its charm or revitalize itself.

A day outdoors

*Did you know… Humans need at least 10–15 minutes of sunlight exposure twice a week to have the vitamin D necessary to sustain good health.**

This morning I was invited to take a nature hike with a local group of birders. It was a beautiful fall day in every way imaginable – brisk breeze, brilliant blue sky, fluffy, picture-perfect clouds and birds galore – bluebirds preparing to fly south together, a lone oriole in some trees along the edge of the prairie, and a stunning whip-poor-will (my first sighting of this mottled brown ground bird ever and in of all places, a post-harvest vegetable garden!). Time flew!

Little did I know, less than five hours later I would meet a teen at the neighbor-hood park who had never taken a hike. Jessica, a 13-year-old girl who attended the local middle school had a glimmer in her eye when I told her that I taken my children for a hike that morning. "I've always wanted to go for a hike," she said. I asked her where she went to elementary school. She told me that she attended elementary school in the same district where she was currently attending middle school, but that she had never gone hiking, not even at outdoor education camp. Apparently, when she went to camp it was too cold to hike and one of the kids was afraid he would have problems breathing (even though he had brought his medicine), so the whole group was kept inside. I could tell she really wanted to go hiking, and urged her to bring her family out to the nature center.

She didn't make it to the free hike that day, but hopefully one day, she and the children she was babysitting will enjoy an autumn hike in the woods, wetland, or prairie with family, friends, or perhaps another naturalist they encounter along the way. No 13-year-old should ever say she hasn't been for a hike, no, not ever.

- ➢ Share nature.

- Support local, regional, national and international nature organizations that offer educational activities for children and open space for everyone.

- Cultivate natural play spaces at home – We have a mud pit in our backyard where a shrub once grew, native wildflowers, and a vegetable garden.

- Volunteer to take families and groups of neighbors out for seasonal nature walks once a week.

**Source: Brender E, Burke A, & Glass RM (2005). Journal of the American Medical Association, 294(18): 2386. National Environmental Foundation*

Take a walk with family and friends

Explore local natural areas with family and friends. Reflect on ways that sharing experiences in nature enrich you, your family, and friendships. List practical ways you can get out in nature more often and bring others with you.

Example: I will get more friends out in nature by inviting them to hike with me once a month.

____

____

____

____

____

____

____

Good all around

Did you know... The word "faith" comes from the Latin root "fidere", which means to trust.

Inspiration can be found anytime anywhere – from the first rays of light at dawn to the darkest nights. Maybe it's the contrast of light with darkness that parallels our own lives – the essence of being that catches our eye or tugs at our heart, if but for a fleeting moment, to be tucked into memories.

What if you could experience the depth of something eternal wherever you were -- in town, watching the kaleidoscope of humanity passing by; in the backyard, beholding a bee gathering pollen; in an airplane flying above mounds of clouds, or swimming in the deepest parts of the sea? Faith and spiritual experiences should be as common as the grains of sand in a desert.

- ➢ Challenge yourself to see the larger picture, something greater than any of us at work, something GOOD – call it God, Spirit or whatever title fits your way of thinking.

- Acknowledge the beauty of the natural world that you have been entrusted to protect.

- Preserve nature in your community.

- Share your love of nature with others.

Give thanks for good things happening in your community, work or life.

____

____

____

____

____

____

____

Resources

Here are a few great sources of information, activities, and support for adventures everyday. Enjoy!

Sustainable community building

- The National Center for Bicycling and Walking, www.bikewalk.org.

Birds

- Cornell Lab of Ornithology
  http://www.birds.cornell.edu/netcommunity/Page.aspx?pid=1478

- National Audubon Society
  http://web4.audubon.org/bird/boa/boa_index.html

- University of Maine Cooperative Extension – "Bird Feeding Basics"
  http://umaine.edu/publications/7124e/

Composting

- Composting and Mulching: A Guide to Managing Organic Yard Waste:
  http://www.extension.umn.edu/distribution/horticulture/DG3296.html

- Don't bag it, Compost it!!
  http://aggie-horticulture.tamu.edu/publications/landscape/compost/

Gardening

- Starting a community garden
  http://communitygarden.org/learn/starting-a-community-garden.php

- Companion planting http://attra.ncat.org/attra-pub/complant.html

- Plant a Row for the Hungry https://gardenwriters.org/Par

Gleaning

- USDA: A Citizen's Guide to Food Recovery
  http://www.usda.gov/news/pubs/gleaning/content.htm

- USDA "Best Practices" Manual: Food Recovery & Gleaning
  http://www.fns.usda.gov/fdd/gleaning/gleanintro.htm

Native landscaping

- US EPA, Landscaping with Native Plants
  http://www.epa.gov/greenacres/navland.html

- Wild Ones http://www.for-wild.org/

- Rain Gardens a How-To Manual for Homeowners
  http://learningstore.uwex.edu/assets/pdfs/GWQ037.pdf

- Gray water information
  http://www.sahra.arizona.edu/programs/water_cons/tips/re-use/gray.htm

Natural area preservation and protection

- International Dark-Sky Association http://www.darksky.org/

- Living Lands and Waters http://www.livinglandsandwaters.org/

- The Nature Conservancy http://www.nature.org/

Nature crafts

- National Wildlife Federation http://www.nwf.org/getgreen/tips

- All Free Crafts http://www.allfreecrafts.com

Outdoor activities for youth and families

- American Camping Association
  http://www.campparents.org/nature/family-fun

- Children & Nature Network http://www.childrenandnature.org/

- National Wildlife Federation Green Hour

Recycling

- Container Recycling Institute www.container-recycling.org

- Freecycle.org for computer-savvy people to connect

- Thrift shops keep clothing, furniture, and other gently used items out of landfills while providing employment opportunities and financial resources to organizations doing positive things in your community. Do a web search where you live for the nearest thrift shop or ask a friend.

- Habitat for Humanity – ReStore
  http://www.habitat.org/env/restores.aspx

- Recycle plastic water caps with
  Aveda http://www.aveda.com/aboutaveda/caps.tmpl

- *Rubbish!: The Archeology of Garbage* by William Rathjie and Cullen Murphy.

Wildlife protection

- Wildlife rehabilitators by zip code http://www.wildliferehabber.org/

- National Wildlife Rehabilitators Association
  http://www.nwrawildlife.org/page.asp?ID=214

- The Humane Society of the United States, Suggestions for Driving with Wildlife

Suggested readings

- *On Meadowview Street* by Henry Cole

- *Acres of Diamonds* by Russell Conwell

- *The Greatest Thing in the World* by Henry Drummond

- *The New Art of Living* by Norman Vincent Peale

- *From the Bottom Up: Man's Crusade to Clean America's Rivers* by Chad Pregracke

- *The Carrot Seed* by Ruth Krauss

- *The Fall of Freddie the Leaf* by Leo Buscaglia, PhD

- *The Secret* by Rhonda Byrne

- *The Road Not Taken* (poem) Robert Frost